"Once in a while one comes across a book which effectively 'stirs up the gift within,' and unmistakably bears the imprimatur of the Holy Spirit of God. Paul E. Billheimer in **Destined for the Throne** has given the evangelical world such a book . One cannot read the author's insights without being challenged and blessed. Buttressing his discussion with Scripture, he has brought us things 'new and old,' but with a freshness which puts flesh in its place, and puts Christ on the throne." Lee Fisher, Billy Graham Association.

"This book is not for those satisfied with cradles and pacifiers. But for others yearning to be more useful in our Master's service, here is a meaty volume of practical value. It is lucid, perceptive, and alive. Too many authors merely "saw sawdust." But not this one. After reading **Destined for the Throne** one may well want to keep it near for easy reference." S. I. McMillen, M. D., author.

"The book challenged me to see the Church in all her glory: where we have originated, where we are going in God's eternal purposes. It ties intercession into the why of our existence. I was left with a desire to be who I am in Christ. The current renewal of the Church could do with some deepening in the areas of intercession, and I believe this book could play a part in that." Malcolm Smith, Bible teacher.

And they sung a new song, saying, Thou art worthy to take the book, and to open the seals thereof: for thou wast slain, and hast redeemed us to God by thy blood out of every kindred, and tongue, and people, and nation; and hast made us unto our God kings and priests: and we shall reign on the earth.

— Revelation 5:9,10.

DESTINED FOR THE THRONE

PAUL E. BILLHEIMER

BETHANY HOUSE PUBLISHERS
MINNEAPOLIS, MINNESOTA 55438
A Division of Bethany Fellowship, Inc

CHRISTIAN LITERATURE CRUSADE
Fort Washington, Pennsylvania 19034

Co-published by
Bethany House Publishers and
Christian Literature Crusade

Printed in the United States of America

Library of Congress Cataloging in Publication Data

Billheimer, Paul E.
   Destined for the throne.

   1. Church. 2. Prayer. I. Title.
BV600.2.B52   1983   262'.7   83-15151
ISBN 0-87123-309-6

Quiet Talks on Prayer by S. D. Gordon. Fleming H. Revell Company, Old Tappan, NJ 07675. Used by permission.

Somewhat Less Than God by Leonard Verduin. Wm. B. Eerdmans Publishing Co., Grand Rapids, MI 49502. Used by permission.

Bible Study Guide for Adults (April 14, 1968 material by Dr. Wilbur T. Dayton). General Department of Sunday Schools, The Wesleyan Church, Marion, IN 46952. Used by permission.

To My Wife

For her valuable assistance, not only in transcribing the manuscript, but also in offering valid criticism and appropriate suggestions, this little volume is affectionately dedicated.

My Thanks To

Miss Frances Ashwell, Mrs. Howard Boardman, Mrs. Kellogg Maddox, and Mr. John Weekley for their dedication in typing and reproducing the manuscript for publication.

PREFACE

No system of philosophy or theology is challenge-proof. The contending schools of theology, Calvinism and Arminianism, illustrate this point. Each has its sincere apologists as well as its equally sincere antagonists. Yet each is accepted in large circles as a viable system of truth with much to recommend it.

In the realm of philosophy, no single system offers an adequate explanation of the universe. All fall short of advancing a fully satisfying cause for and interpretation of the meaning of existence. Science, with its tremendous contribution to mundane affairs and to the enrichment of life in general, is of little help here. Apart from the Bible, the universe is an incomprehensible mystery. The Bible alone offers the only satisfactory explanation for the age-old questions ''Who is man?'' ''Why is he here?'' ''What is the meaning of life?''

Many of the theses advanced and expounded in the following pages were, at first, so startlingly unconventional and sometimes so overwhelmingly astounding to the writer as to stagger his imagination and boggle his mind. It may, therefore, not be surprising if others find the viewpoints equally astonishing. Hence, may I urge the reader to carefully consider the insights presented in the light of both Scripture and reason.

Wherever the messages which form these chapters have been given, whether from the pulpit or person-to-person, they have been received with appreciation. I believe the following pages contain a message especially pertinent to this end time. The book is offered to the Church with a sincere prayer that it will make a significant contribution to the spiritual life of the Body and Bride of Christ.

The writer feels that many of the insights were given him by the personal ministry of the Holy Spirit through the Word. He, therefore, relinquishes all claim to ownership. He wishes his ministerial brethren to feel perfectly free to use in their own ministry any material herein which the Spirit may quicken to them, subject only to the terms of the copyright. The truths were given by the Spirit. They belong to the Body.

CONTENTS

FOREWORD

I have just read the manuscript of Paul E. Billheimer's book *Destined for the Throne*, and have been inspired and challenged by the insights and fresh interpretations of the Scriptures regarding prayer, praise, and the church's place in the world. Every Christian who feels impelled to find a deeper dimension of Christian witness should not only read this book, but study it prayerfully, and apply its principles to his life.

BILLY GRAHAM

INTRODUCTION

The following chapters present what some consider a totally new and unique cosmology. The author's primary thesis is that the *one* purpose of the universe from all eternity is the production and preparation of an Eternal Companion for the Son, called the Bride, the Lamb's Wife. Since she is to share the throne of the universe with her Divine Lover and Lord as a judicial equal, she must be trained, educated, and prepared for her queenly role.

Because the crown is only for the conqueror (Rev. 3:21), the Church (later to become the Bride) must learn the art of spiritual warfare, of overcoming evil forces in preparation for her assumption of the throne following the Marriage Supper of the Lamb. To enable her to learn the technique of overcoming, God ordained the infinitely wise program of believing prayer. He did not ordain prayer primarily as a way of getting things done. It is His way of giving the Church "on-the-job" training in overcoming the forces hostile to God. This world is a laboratory in which those destined for the throne are learning in actual practice how to overcome Satan and his hierarchy. The prayer closet is the arena which produces the overcomer.

This means that *redeemed humanity* outranks all other orders of created beings in the universe. Angels are created, not generated. Redeemed humanity is both created and generated, begotten of God, bearing His "genes," His heredity. Through the new birth a redeemed human being becomes a bona fide member of the original cosmic family, "next of kin" to the Trinity. Thus God has exalted redeemed humanity to such a sublime height that it is impossible for Him to elevate them further without breaching the Godhead. This is the basis for the divine accolade of Psalm 8:5: "Thou hast made him but little lower than God" (*ASV and Amplified*).

The Church, through her resurrection and ascension with Christ, is already legally on the throne. Through the use of her weapons of prayer and faith she holds in this present throbbing moment the balance of power in world affairs. In spite of all of her lamentable weaknesses, appalling failures, and indefensible shortcomings, the Church is the mightiest force for civilization and enlightened social consciousness in the world today. The only force that is contesting Satan's total rule in human affairs is the Church of the Living God. If Satan were unopposed, if he were under no restraint generated by the Spirit-inspired prayers and holy lives of God's people, "the pillared firmament itself were rottenness and earth's base built on stubble." "Ye are the salt of the earth . . . . Ye are the light of the world" (Matt. 5:13-14). If it were not for the purifying and preserving influence of the Church on earth, the fabric of all we call civilization would totally disintegrate, decay, and disappear. The fact that the social order has been preserved from total devastation in spite of Satan's worst, proves that at least a remnant of the Church is effectually functioning and already has entered upon her rulership in union with her living Lord. She is, therefore, even now by virtue of the weapons of prayer and faith engaged in "on-the-job" training for her place as co-sovereign with Christ over the entire universe following Satan's final destruction.

The Church, by virtue of her faithful use of prayer, wields the balance of power not only in world affairs but also in the salvation of individual şouls. Without violating the free moral responsibility of any individual, the Church, by means of persistent, believing intercession, may so release the Spirit of God upon a soul that he will find it easier to yield to the Spirit's tender wooing and be saved than to continue his rebellion.

God will not go over the Church's head to do things in spite of her because this would abort His plan to bring her to full stature as co-sovereign with the Son. He will therefore do nothing without her. To this John Wesley agrees when he says, "God does nothing but in answer to prayer."

In order to enable the Church to overcome Satan, God entered the stream of human history in the Incarnation. As unfallen Man He overcame and destroyed Satan both legally and dynamically. All that Christ did in redemption He did for the benefit of the Church. He is "head over all things *to the church*" (Eph. 1:22). His victory over Satan is accredited to the Church. Although Christ's triumph over Satan is full and complete, God permits him to carry on a guerrilla warfare. God could put Satan completely away, but He has chosen to use him to give the Church "on-the-job" training in overcoming.

Prayer is not begging God to do something which He is loath to do. It is not overcoming reluctance in God. It is enforcing Christ's victory over Satan. It is implementing upon earth Heaven's decisions concerning the affairs of men. Calvary legally destroyed Satan, and canceled all of his claims. God placed the enforcement of Calvary's victory in the hands of the Church (Matt. 18:18 and Luke 10:17-19). He has given to her "power of attorney." She is His "deputy." But this delegated authority is wholly inoperative apart from the prayers of a believing Church. Therefore, prayer is where the action is. Any church without a well-organized and systematic prayer program is simply operating a religious treadmill.

A program of prayer without faith is powerless. The missing element that is necessary to energize prevailing prayer that binds and casts out Satan is triumphant faith. And the missing element that is necessary to energize triumphant faith is praise—perpetual, purposeful, aggressive praise. Praise is the highest form of prayer because it combines petition with faith. Praise is the spark plug of faith. It is the one thing needed to get faith airborne, enabling it to soar above the deadly miasma of doubt. Praise is the detergent which purifies faith and purges doubt from the heart. The secret of answered prayer is faith without doubt (Mark 11:23). And the secret of faith without doubt is praise, triumphant praise, continuous praise, praise that is a way of life. This is the solution to the problem of a living faith and successful prayer.

The secret of success in overcoming Satan and qualifying for the throne is a massive program of effective prayer. The secret of effective prayer is a massive program of praise.

These and other theses are expounded and amplified in the pages of this book.

1

THE ULTIMATE GOAL OF THE UNIVERSE: THE CHURCH

God is the Lord of History

Few secular historians have any conception of the meaning and purpose of history. They may be able to record and systematize the characters and events which allegedly comprise its raw material, but they have little or no clue to their interpretation or significance. This is admitted by some noted historians themselves. G. N. Clark, for instance, in his inaugural address at Cambridge, said, "There is no secret and no plan in history to be discovered." Andre Maurois, French biographer, critic, and novelist opines, "The universe is indifferent. Who created it? Why are we here on this puny mud heap spinning in infinite space? I have not the slightest idea and I am quite convinced no one has . . . ." Other authorities who may be less candid are equally perplexed concerning the purpose and motive of the events and characters which they record and describe.

Existence an Impenetrable Mystery to the Ancients

The ancient Greeks considered history as a circle or a cycle, always repeating itself, therefore going nowhere in particular, accomplishing no discernible purpose, and without an identifiable goal. To them existence was an impenetrable mystery. And this is the philosophy embraced and expounded by most modern secular chroniclers. They do not know what existence is about. To them and to much of the world at large, history is merely one senseless crisis after another and has no purpose and no intelligent aim. They do not know the reason for intelligent life or for the existence of the human race. They do not know where we came from or where we are going. All being is a vast incomprehensible enigma. Their philosophy of history is a philosophy of ignorance, frustration, and despair.

The Universe Purposeless to Moderns

In modern times this philosophy was popularized by a Frenchman named Jean Paul Sartre, who taught that each man exists in a watertight compartment as an isolated individual in a purposeless universe. Since we cannot know who we are, where we came from, and where we are going; since we do not understand the past and have no hope of the future, then the present throbbing moment is all that matters. Only what we realize in the immediate present is significant and has meaning. Distant goals have no validity. Therefore, to sacrifice the present for the future is nonsensical and stupid. Out of this philosophy came the "now generation," the generation which cannot wait. The pleasure of the moment is the only rational goal of existence. "On with the dance, let joy be unconfined." "Let us eat and drink; for tomorrow we die" (1 Cor. 15:32).

A generation of college youth steeped in this existential philosophy of license, futility, and despair naturally erupted in revolutionary violence, arson, and rapine, spreading death and destruction in cities and on college campuses throughout the nation and the world. Almost overnight society exploded in lawlessness and crime, rioting and murder, and in the insanity of the drug culture. This was the result of the philosophy of ignorance concerning the past and hopelessness concerning the future.[1]

The Bible — The Only Infallible Source Book

The average historian has no clue to the meaning of history because he ignores the only infallible source book, the Bible. For most people, historians included, the center of history for any given age or period is the political entity or state which is the most populous, which occupies the greatest territory, represents supreme material resources, and boasts the largest and most invincible military might. To most of us, the stuff of history is the part played by the great empires of the past, including the leading political, military, and financial figures associated with them. So men like the Pharaohs, Nebuchadnezzar, Alexander the Great, Caesar, Charlemagne, and Napoleon seem to be the authentic makers of history. These empire builders and their followers considered themselves to be the architects of fate and the molders of destiny. They believed that they were the central forces of history, and the prime movers of its events.

Calvary — The True Center of History

But the world at large and its historians in particular have missed the point altogether. There is only one philosophy of history that makes sense and that is the Biblical philosophy.[2]

The center of history is not its great empires like Egypt, Babylon, Greece, or Rome, nor their modern counterparts such as Russia, China, the United States of America, or any other which may yet appear. To locate the center of history one must bypass all these vast empires and the glittering names associated with them and find his way to a tiny land called the navel of the earth, the geographical center of the world. And in that tiny land is a tiny hill called Calvary, where two thousand years ago a Man named Jesus was lifted up to die. And this writer submits that that tiny hill in that tiny land is the center of all history, not only of this world, but of all the countless galaxies and island universes of outer space from eternity to eternity.

The Church — The Central Object and Goal of History

This Man hanging upon that bloody cross amid the taunts and jeers of the passers by was *"before all things"* (Col. 1:17), that is, before history itself. He is the starting point of history, for "all things were made by him; and without him was not anything made that was made" (John 1:3). And the history that began in Him was and is fashioned and controlled by Him. "He regulates the universe by the mighty power of his command" (Heb. 1:3 *Living Bible*]. And it was and is fashioned and controlled by Him with a single specific purpose in view. That specific purpose and design is always the central and controlling factor of history no matter how wide its sweep may be.

Every event in history transpires to serve that purpose. Nothing, no matter how small, is excluded. The universe, including this planet, was created for one purpose: to provide a suitable habitation for the human race.[3] The human race was created in the image and likeness of God for one purpose: to provide an eternal companion for the Son. After the fall and promise of redemption through the coming Messiah, the Messianic race was born and nurtured in order to bring in the Messiah. And the Messiah came for one intent and only one: to give birth to His Church, thus to obtain His Bride. The Church, then—the called-out body of redeemed mankind—turns out to be the central object, the goal, not only of mundane history but of all that God has been doing in all realms, from all eternity.

If this is true, then all history is sacred. There is no such thing as secular history. So history is simply "His story." The entire universe in its totality is cooperating with God in His purpose to select and train His Church as His

Eternal Companion. The entire universe is ordered for this purpose, for all things belong to the Church and are for her benefit (1 Cor. 3:21-23). As the *Lord of history,* God is controlling all of its events, not only on earth but in all realms, to serve His purpose of bringing to maturity and eventually to enthronement with His Son, not angels or archangels, but the Church, His chosen Bride.[4] This was the glorious truth revealed to Paul when he wrote: "We know that all things [the entire cosmos] work together [are cooperating] for good to them that love God [the Church], to them who are the called according to his purpose [the Bride]" (Rom. 8:28).

Romance at the Heart of the Universe

From this it is implicit that romance is at the heart of the universe and is the key to all existence. From all eternity God purposed that at some time in the future His Son should have an Eternal Companion, described by John the Revelator as "the bride, the Lamb's wife" (Rev. 21:9). John further revealed that this Eternal Companion in God's eternal purpose is to share the Bridegroom's throne following the Marriage Supper of the Lamb (Rev. 3:21). Here we see the ultimate purpose, the climactic goal of history.

According to Romans 8:28 this is the total objective, the single, solitary motive of all God's creative acts. This passage teaches clearly that all that God has been doing from the very beginning was focused upon the Church. This, and this alone, fully unveils the mystery of history and makes it understandable.[5] No secular historian can be expected to comprehend this. But if our understanding of Romans 8:28 is true, then for the Church "suns and moons wax and wane"; for her, starry galaxies pile the heavens; for her, island universes swing in outer space; for her, earthly kingdoms rise and fall. (Psalm 75:6-7 and Psalm 105).

Therefore it was not for their own intrinsic importance that Pharaoh, Nebuchadnezzar, Darius, Sennacherib and others were raised up. This is the gist of Isaiah 10:5-14 [*LB*]. These kings derived their significance wholly from their relationship to God's purpose for the Messianic nation, through whom the Messiah was to come. Some day we will understand that not only these Biblically recorded instances but all events from all eternity were ordered and directed for one purpose and one alone — the eventual winning and preparation of the Bride.

In his *Bible Handbook* (New Revised Edition, page 20), Henry Halley has pointed out that

> . . . the Old Testament is the account of a nation. The New Testament is the account of a MAN. The Nation was founded and nurtured of God to bring the Man into the world.*

But what was the purpose of the Man? He came to die — to die and rise again (John 12:27). And what then was the purpose of that? The conventional answer is that He died and rose again to redeem the world.

Limited Acceptance of an Unlimited Atonement

You may be surprised when I say that in my opinion this answer is too simplistic, that it fails to encompass all the factors involved. It is true that His death and resurrection did provide for the redemption of *all* mankind. Not one soul of Adam's race was excluded. "And he is the propitiation for our sins, and not for ours only, but also for the sins of the *whole world*" (1 John 2:2). All that have been or ever will be born from the dawn of human history to the dawn of eternal ages are included in God's all-embracing redemptive love. But God knew from the very beginning that only a select remnant would accept this universal provision. This is clearly revealed by Jesus Himself in Matthew 7:13-14: ''Wide is the gate and broad is the way that leadeth to destruction, and many there be who go in thereat; because strait is the gate and narrow is the way that leadeth unto life, and *few* there be that find it.''

If God knew from all eternity that the net result of all His creative activity, including the plan of redemption, would be only this tiny minority, comparatively speaking, then it may be presumed that this small group was the object of all of God's previous plans, purposes, and creative enterprises.[6] *Therefore, it follows that it was for the sake of this small group that the universe was originated.* It was for them that the inhabitants of outer space, the unseen world, were brought into being (Heb. 1:14). It was for them that the earth and the world were formed. For their sake the Adamic race was born. To possess them, God Himself entered the stream of history in the Incarnation. And this small group is called the Church; the Bride, the Lamb's Wife (Matt. 16:18, Rev. 21:9).[7]

The Bride — The Finished Product of the Ages

This view is further strengthened by what may be called ''the residual argument.''[8] If one wants to know the meaning and purpose of history, he must look at the end, the final outcome, the net result. Since prophecy is history written in advance, we have history's final chapter in the Book of Revelation. Turning to the closing pages, what emerges as the finished product of the ages? It is one thing and one alone: *the Eternal Companion of the God-Man.* The final and ultimate outcome and goal of events from eternity to eternity, the finished product of all the ages, is the spotless Bride of Christ, united with Him in wedded bliss at the Marriage Supper of the Lamb and seated with her heavenly Bridegroom upon the throne of the universe

— ruling and reigning with Him over an ever increasing and expanding Kingdom. He entered the stream of human history for this one purpose, to claim His Beloved (Rev. 19:6,9; 21:7, 9, 10).

Thus the Church, and only the Church, is the key to and explanation of history. The Church, blood-washed and spotless, is the center, the reason, and the goal of all of God's vast creative handiwork. Therefore, history is only the handmaiden of the Church, and the nations of the world are but puppets manipulated by God for the purposes of His Church (Acts 17:26). *Creation has no other aim. History has no other goal.* From before the foundation of the world until the dawn of eternal ages God has been working toward one grand event, one supreme end — the glorious wedding of His Son, the Marriage Supper of the Lamb.

The Celestial Wedding and the Beginning of God's Eternal Enterprise

As in the case of Adam, God saw that it was not good for His Son to be alone. From the very beginning it was God's plan and purpose that out of the riven side of His Son should come an Eternal Companion to sit by His side upon the throne of the universe as a bona fide partner, a judicial equal,[9] to share with Him His sovereign power and authority over His eternal kingdom. "Fear not, little flock, for it is your Father's good pleasure to give you the kingdom" (Luke 12:32). "To him that overcometh will I grant to sit with me in my throne, even as I also overcame and am set down with my Father in his throne" (Rev. 3:21).

To be given the kingdom is more than to internalize kingdom principles and ethics. That is only one phase of it. To be given a kingdom is to be made a king, to be invested with authority over a kingdom. That this is God's glorious purpose for the Church is authenticated and confirmed by

Paul in 1 Corinthians 6:2-3: "Do ye not know that the saints shall judge the world? . . . Know ye not that we shall judge angels?" This is an *earnest* of what Jesus meant when He said, "The glory that thou gavest me I have given them" (John 17:22).

This royalty and rulership is no hollow, empty, figurative, symbolical, or emblematic thing. It is not a figment of the imagination. The Church, the Bride, the Eternal Companion is to sit *with Him* on His throne. If His throne represents reality, then hers is no fantasy. Neither joint heir can do anything alone (Rom. 8:17).

We may not know why it pleases the Father to give the kingdom to the little flock. We may not know why Christ chooses to share His throne and His glory with the redeemed. We only know that He *has chosen* to do so and that it gives Him pleasure.

Therefore, from all eternity, all that precedes the Marriage Supper of the Lamb is preliminary and preparatory. Only thereafter will God's program for the eternal ages begin to unfold. God will not be ready, so to speak, to enter upon His ultimate and supreme enterprise for the ages until the Bride is on the throne with her divine Lover and Lord. Up until then, the entire universe under the Son's regulation and control is being manipulated by God for one purpose — *to prepare and train the Bride.* Verily, God is the Lord of history.

NOTES

1. This philosophy of ignorance conerning the past and hopelessness concerning the future is echoed and emphasized in the view of some modern biologists and psychologists. In his book *Chance and Necessity* Jacques Monod, the French molecular biologist, argues that man's existence is due to the chance collision between miniscule particles of nucleic acid and proteins in the vast "pre-biotic soup." According to Dr. Francis Schaeffer's quotation from *Newsweek* magazine in *Back to Freedom and Dignity,* Monod holds that "all life results from interaction of pure chance — and necessity." Monod concludes that man is alone (as far as a Superior Being is concerned) in the universe's unfeeling immensity, out of which he emerged only by chance. His destiny is nowhere spelled out, nor is his duty. As expressed in Dr. Schaeffer's book, Monod is convinced that "man is the product of the impersonal, plus time, plus chance."

If this is true, then man is as impersonal as and has no more value than any other part of the universe. There is, therefore, no moral distinction between cutting down a tree and destroying a human being. If a human being is essentially no different from a tree, then his future is no different. Existence, for a man, is as meaningless as existence for a tree; thus man's value is reduced to zero. The end result is meaninglessness and despair. According to Dr. Schaeffer, this is what triggered the student rebellion at Berkeley, and, one might conclude, on many other campuses throughout our nation and the world. When man destroys God, he destroys himself. *Atheism is suicidal.*

2. This viewpoint is ably expressed by Erich Sauer: "As the Creator of the course of history and Governor of heaven and earth He [God] controls the universal process. Therefore, as the Lord of history, He and He alone, can explain history . . . . Therefore, the Bible is the

'Book of mankind' — the key to world events. All understanding to
the whole of human affairs depends upon the attitude to it'' (From
Eternity to Eternity, page 97).

"All history is incomprehensible without Christ" (Ernest Renan).

3. All conservative exposition agrees that the scriptural account of
creation emphasizes that man is the goal and crown of the creation
process. Even Nietzsche said, ''Man is the reason for the world''
(Erich Sauer in *The King of the Earth,* page 49).

Concerning the Genesis account of creation, Leonard Verduin
says, ''The plain implication is that from the earliest beginnings the
divine interest was to reach its climax in man. All that goes before is
anticipatory, propaedeutic to the dominion-haver known as man.
Man is pictured as the crown and capstone of the entire creative
enterprise of the Almighty; man is the goal toward which the whole
undertaking moved. Verily, the Bible does not speak meanly of man''
(*Somewhat Less Than God,* Page 9).

4. Watchman Nee points out that the church is now the body of
Christ but will be His Bride after the Marriage Supper of the Lamb
(*The Glorious Church,* Chapter 3, page 46, 1968 edition).

5. The thesis of this section has been challenged on the ground
''that too much is being built on one verse out of context.''

The author recognizes the validity of this criticism since the word
translated ''all things'' in Romans 8:28 is not the word used for the
cosmos elsewhere.

The claim that if *some* events are working for the good of the
Church then *all in the entire universe* must also be working to that
end, is a necessary and incontestable corollary of the doctrine of
monotheism.

If there is only one God and He is supreme, then all of His purposes
and acts are coordinated and are directed to one and the same end.
Only if there is a rival power or divided authority could there be cross
currents or purposes. This would produce chaos. Therefore, if there
is one supreme God in the universe, then the universe is a cosmos.
If the universe is a cosmos, a harmonious and ordered whole, then all
circumstances and events in the cosmos are working toward one and
the same end.

That the universe is a cosmos, under the control of one supreme
authority, is taught by such passages as Psalm 103:19, ''The Lord
hath prepared his throne in the heavens, and his kingdom ruleth over

all.'' This truth is the theme of much of the Psalms and prophets, and runs throughout all Scripture from Genesis to Revelation. This means that the entire universe is one ordered whole, a harmonious unit, a cosmos.

In such a universe under the control of a central absolute authority, if one event or series of events is working for the good of the Church, then all events are serving the same purpose.

A clear example of the cosmos cooperating in God's Messianic purpose, and therefore in His purpose for the Church, is found in Judges 5:20, ''The stars in their courses fought against Sisera.'' Many other passages illustrate this same point.

Therefore, the ''all things'' of Romans 8:28 includes not only certain limited particulars, but the sum total of all that is included in the universe.

6. The writer believes that the redeemed are innumerable (Rev. 7:9). The terms ''small group'' and ''tiny minority'' are used comparatively of those who exercised, or will exercise, freedom of choice during the day of salvation. If the untold millions who died or will die in infancy and prenatally are included in the redeemed, as we believe, it is true as has been said, ''that ultimately the lost shall bear to the saved no greater proportion than the inmates of a prison do to the mass of the community.''

7. The writer believes that the Church includes all the redeemed from creation to eternity.

8. The automobile industry provides an illuminating illustration of what has been termed ''the residual argument.'' The automobile was once but a concept, an idea, a dream in the mind of a man. But that idea gave rise to a great enterprise. To manufacture the automobile, huge building complexes covering thousands of acres of land have been erected at astronomical cost. These plants have been filled with sophisticated machines, tools, and equipment involving enormous amounts of capital. The operation requires limitless raw materials of many kinds from around the world in proportions that stagger the imagination. These industrial complexes employ millions of men and women from engineers to assembly line operators. And all of this for one purpose and one alone: a tiny automobile. When that first small vehicle comes from the assembly line, the purpose of this vast conglomerate of industries becomes perfectly clear. All that has gone before, including the huge outlay, the processing of raw material with its resultant wastes in huge amounts, everything from the drawing

board to the last bolt is illuminated and explained by one thing and one alone: the existence of a motor car. That small vehicle is the key that unlocks the mystery of all that has preceded.

9. Judicial — "allowed, enforced or set by order of a judge or law court" (*Webster's New World Dictionary*). The equality which is here in view is a delegated equality. Although it is a delegated equality, *it is as fully recognized and respected as if it were original.* This delegated equality is unimistakably implied in the term "joint heir" (Rom. 8:17). In law a joint heir can do nothing alone, nothing without the other.

2

GOD'S PURPOSE FOR THE CHURCH: SUPREME RANK

Supreme Rank of Redeemed Humanity

It must be clear from the preceding chapter that redeemed humanity occupies a totally unique position in the hierarchy of the universe. This is no attempt to depreciate the rank of angels or to bedim the radiant splendor of their glory. They are indescribably beautiful, unspeakably majestic, unutterably powerful, and supernaturally intelligent. They rule celestial domains of untold magnitude and of inconceivable grandeur. Their dazzling rank is further attested by the fact that they surround the throne of the Almighty and constitute the court of the King of kings. Exalted as they are, however, the highest ranking angel hovering over the throne of the Most High is outranked — wonder of wonders — by the most insignificant human being who has been born again, redeemed by the blood of the Lamb.

God "Tipped His Hand" in the Incarnation

Created originally in the image of God, redeemed humanity has been elevated by means of a *divinely conceived genetic process* known as the new birth to the highest rank of all created beings. ''He took not on him the nature of angels, but he took on him the seed of Abraham'' (Heb. 2:16). However else He might manifest Himself in nature, God could not become *incarnate* in angels because they were not created in the full image of God.[1] No other created being approaches the capacity of the human being to "contain and utter God." Only man has a nature in which God can become incarnate. God "tipped His hand," so to speak, in the Incarnation. By this He dignified the human race and elevated redeemed humanity beyond the highest ranking angelic star in the radiant canopy of the firmament.

Angels Created—Not Generated

Because angels were not made in the image of God and God could therefore not become incarnate in them, the fallen angels cannot be redeemed. No angel can ever become a congenital member of the family of God. They are created, not generated, beings; therefore, no angel can become a blood-born son of God. Angels can never have the heritage, the "genes" of God. They can never be partakers of the divine nature.

None can ever become a member of the Bridehood. These marks of privilege and rank have been reserved for redeemed humanity alone.

Which of the angels has been privileged to say "Behold what manner of love the Father hath bestowed upon *us* that *we* should be called the [generic] sons of God"? Or, "When he shall appear *we* shall be like him"? (1 John 3:1,2). Hebrews 2:11 says, "For both he that sanctifieth and they who are sanctified are all of one [origin], for which cause he is not ashamed to call them brethren." To which of the angels said He at any time, "You are my brother or sister or mother"? that is, "We are all of one origin, we have been begotten by the same Father"? (Matt. 12:48-50). Did He ever say of the angels as He said of His disciples, "That they all may be one; as thou, Father, art in me, and I in thee, that they also may be one in us . . . that they may be one, even as we are one . . . I in them, and thou in me, that they may be made perfect in one . . ."?

(John 17:21-23). Did Paul ever say of the angels as he did of the Church, that they constitute His Body of which He is the Head, "the fullness of him that filleth all in all"? (Eph. 1:23). Did Paul say to angels, or to the Church, "[Ye] are members of his body, of his flesh, and of his bones"? (Eph. 5:30).

The Redeemed an "Extension" of the Godhead

But this is not all. We tread softly here. With bated breath we read in 1 Corinthians 6:17: "He that is joined to the Lord is one spirit." This union goes beyond a mere formal, functional, or idealistic harmony or rapport. It is an organic unity, an "organic relationship of personalities" (Sauer). Through the new birth we become bona fide members of the original cosmic family (Eph. 3:15), actual generated sons of God (1 John 3:2), "partakers of the divine nature" (2 Peter 1:4), begotten by Him, impregnated with His "genes",* called the seed or "sperma" of God (1 John 5:1,18 and 1 Peter 1:3,23), and bearing His heredity. Thus, through the new birth — and I speak reverently — we become the "next of kin" to the Trinity, a kind of "extension" of the Godhead. That this group outranks all other orders of created beings is attested by Paul's dramatic questions in 1 Corinthians 6:2-3: "Don't you know that some day we Christians are going to judge and govern the world? . . . Don't you realize that we Christians will judge and reward the very angels in heaven?" (*LB*).

The New Species

Here is a completely new, unique, and exclusive order of beings which may be called a "new species." *There is nothing like it in all the kingdoms of infinity.* This is the order of beings which God envisioned when He spoke the worlds into being. This is the order of beings which Paul

---

*No physical relationship is implied

called "the new man" (Eph. 2:15), the "new humanity" destined through the new birth to be the aristocracy of the universe. They form a new and exclusive royalty, a new ruling hierarchy who will also constitute the Bride, the Lamb's Wife. This order is divinely designated to be co-ruler, co-sovereign, co-administrator and a judicially (see Chap. 1, Note 9) equal partner to the throne by virtue of redemption and wedlock with the King of kings.

A Congenital Family Circle

Nothing can ever dim the fact that infinity separates the Creator from the created. Christ is the eternally unique and only begotten Son, "the brightness of [God's] glory," and "the express image of his person" (Heb. 1:3). But from all eternity God purposed to have a family circle of His *very own,* not only created but *also generated* by His own life, incorporating His own seed, "sperma," "genes," or heredity. "Long ago, even before he made the world, God chose us to be *his very own* [in a genetic sense], through what Christ would do for us" (Eph. 1:4; also 5:25-27, 32 *LB*). In order to obtain this personal, organic family relationship, God conceived the infinitely vast and infinitely wise plan of creation *plus* redemption through the new birth, in order to bring "many sons to glory" (Heb. 2:10). "For from the very beginning God decided that those who came to him . . . should become like his Son so that his Son would be the First, with many brothers" (Rom. 8:29 *LB*). In other words, Christ is the Prototype after which all other sons are being fashioned. In John 1:12-13 we learn that the plan of redemption was inaugurated to set up *a unique and original generative method* by which these "many sons" would be born and progressively disciplined by a sanctifying process in order to bring them to glory. "But as many as received him, to them gave he the power to become the sons of God, even to them that believe on his name; who were born, not of blood, nor of the will of the flesh, nor of the will of man, but of God" (John 1:12-13). *Here is a distinct reference to two parallel generative methods, one human, the other divine.* In and through Christ alone does God realize and fulfill His paternal longing for a generic family relationship. *But for this plan, God's family relationship would have been forever confined to the Trinity.*

Princes of the Realm

Those who have worked on an assembly line know that a prototype is first designed, handcrafted, and tested before it is committed to the assembly line. They also know that the purpose of the assembly line is to produce exact duplicates, perfect copies of the original. This is God's purpose in the plan of redemption — to produce, by means of the new birth, an entirely new and unique species, exact replicas of His Son with whom He will share His glory and His dominion, and who will constitute a royal progeny and form the governing and administrative staff of His eternal kingdom.

While we recognize the infinite distinction between the Eternal Son and the "many sons" born into the family, yet such is their heredity as the result of the new birth that He recognizes them as bona fide blood-brothers. And according to 1 John 3:2 that is just what they are, true genetic sons of God and therefore blood-brothers of the Son. Christ is the divine Prototype after which this new species is being made. They are to be exact copies of Him, true genotypes, *as utterly like Him as it is possible for the finite to be like the Infinite.* As sons of God, begotten by Him, incorporating into their fundamental being and nature the very "genes" of God, they rank above all other created beings and are elevated to the most sublime height possible short of becoming members of the Trinity itself. Although Christ is the unique and only begotten Eternal Son, yet *He does not retain His glory for Himself alone* for

He has declared, "The glory which thou gavest me, I have given them" (John 17:22). Therefore, the redeemed will share His glory, His rulership, and His dominion as truly responsible princes of the Realm.

"But Little Lower Than God" (Psalm 8:5 ASV)

By these means God has exalted redeemed humanity to such a sublime rank that it is impossible for Him to elevate them any further without bringing them into the inner circle of the Godhead itself. In the Beloved we have been accepted into the very bosom of the Father (John 1:18), and by virtue of our union with Christ we are accepted upon the same terms as He (Eph. 1:6 and John 17:23). As bona fide sons, generated by the very life of God Himself, as full blood-brothers of the Eternal Son, as members of His Body of which He is the Head, and, as spirit of His Spirit, how can we ever be brought nearer? This mystery has been happily expressed by Rees Howells:

> So nigh, so very nigh to God, I cannot nearer be;
> For in the Person of His Son, I am as near as He.

This agrees with the sublime accolade of Psalm 8:4-5: "What is man, that thou art mindful of him? And the son of man, that thou visitest him [in the Incarnation]? For thou has made him but little lower than God." According to recognized authority, this is the correct translation, since the term used in the original Hebrew is *Elohim*, the first of the names of deity (Gen. 1:1).

Not Megalomania

This brings us to such dizzy heights as to merit the charge, not only of megalomania (illusions of grandeur), not only of hyperbole, but of blasphemy itself, if these conclusions are invalid. *God has exhausted human language to open our eyes to the immensity of His plan for the redeemed.* Unless the words of inspiration are meaningless, the preceding is no exaggeration. "Eye hath not seen, nor ear heard, neither have entered into the heart of man, the things which God hath prepared for them that love him" (1 Cor. 2:9). Hallelujah!

So unspeakably astonishing is the magnitude of God's plan that Paul is constrained to most earnest intercession on our behalf: "I pray that your hearts will be flooded with light so that you can see something of the future he has called you to share" (Eph. 1:18 *LB*). Paul realized that only the illumination of the Holy Spirit can impart even a vague conception of the supreme rank of the redeemed as the "next of kin" to God. Only a divinely inspired faith can faintly comprehend the psalmist's phrase, "but little less than God."

Not Fantasy

Although the inspired words of the Biblical vocabulary are so pregnant with unequivocal meaning, the natural mind is overwhelmed by their implications and is tempted to qualify them by treating them as fantasy, purely as symbols, or as figures of speech. This is the way unbelief frequently emasculates the Word of God. One rule of Biblical interpretation holds that the Word must be accepted literally unless it is clearly figurative or symbolical. Doubtless the reality behind the Biblical terms is far beyond the capacity of human imagination, *yet these terms are valid as far as the mind can comprehend.* To accept them as less than a faithful representation of heavenly reality is to rob them of their content. They were meant to be accepted, not as fantasy, but literally. Therefore, in God's eternal vocabulary, the rank of the redeemed is literally and truthfully "but little less than God."

Relationship Between Rank and Prayer

Perhaps some are wondering what is the relationship of

the supreme rank of the redeemed to the subject of prayer and intercession. *The explanation is that prayer is not primarily God's way of getting things done. It is God's way of giving the Church "on-the-job" training in overcoming the forces hostile to God.* This world is a laboratory in which those destined for the throne are learning, by actual practice in the prayer closet, how to overcome Satan and his hierarchy. *God designed the program of prayer as an "apprenticeship" for eternal sovereignty with Christ.* Here we are learning "the trick of the tools" — how to use the weapons of prayer and faith in overcoming and enforcing Christ's victory so dearly bought. What foes will be left to overcome in the eternal ages we do not know. But the character acquired in overcoming here will evidently be needed when we have joined the Bridegroom on His throne. "To him that *overcometh* will I grant to sit with me in my throne" (Rev. 3:21). "The crown is only for the conqueror" (Sauer). And the conqueror overcomes within the framework of God's program of prayer and faith. *The prayer closet is the arena which produces the overcomer.*

NOTES

1.   There is a clear and convincing implication in Genesis 1:27 that sex, in its spiritual dimension, constitutes an element of the image of God. If sex in its spiritual dimension is a part of that image in which man was created, then it follows that angels were not created in the image of God, whatever other attributes they may have in common with man, i.e., spirit nature; intellectual, emotional, and moral endowments; original holiness. See also Ephesians 5:22-32.

3

THE MYSTERY OF PRAYER

And I sought for a man among them, that should make up the hedge, and stand in the gap before me for the land, that I should not destroy it; but I found none. Therefore have I poured out mine indignation upon them; I have consumed them with the fire of my wrath; their own way have I recompensed upon their heads, saith the Lord God. (Ezekiel 22:30-31).

Prayer a Divine Mystery

Has it ever occured to you that the design of prayer in the divine economy is a fantastically puzzling mystery? Why should there be a system or plan of prayer at all? Is not God almighty and self-sufficient? Could He possibly need any help outside of Himself? Self-sufficiency is one of the attributes of God. Does He need anything which man or any other of His creatures can supply? Could not He who spoke the worlds into existence and who upholds them by that same word accomplish His purposes without the help of puny man? then *why* did He devise the plan of prayer? Why and how did He become ''dependent'' upon the intercession of men? Why can He do nothing in the realm of human redemption apart from human cooperation through prayer and faith? How did He get Himself into such a ''fix''? When God is wholly self-sufficient — when

He, by His will and spoken word, can accomplish any conceivable end — why does He not arbitrarily and without reference to any other being or intelligence or will, proceed to speak the word?

God "Helpless" Without a Man

The mystery of the design of prayer is pointed up in Ezekiel 22:30-31. During a time of national apostasy, God said, "And I sought for a man among them, that should make up the hedge, and stand in the gap before me for the land, that I should not destroy it; but I found none. Therefore have I poured out mine indignation upon them; I have consumed them with the fire of my wrath; and their own way have I recompensed upon their heads."

Here we see God seeking to avoid exercising just and deserved judgment. He, Himself, longs to spare the nation. But, strangely, He is "helpless" without a man, without an intercessor. If no one will intercede, God cannot withhold judgment. *Why* should He be "dependent" upon the prayers of a man to defend the nation from the judgments which He, Himself, wishes to withhold? God is the almighty and supreme Sovereign of the universe. He is Himself the ultimate Judge, Jury, and Executive and Enforcement Authority. *Or is He?* If He longed to withhold judgment against His people, if He yearned to show mercy, why did He not exercise His supreme sovereignty and do so, regardless of the prayers — or lack of prayers — of any man? Moreover, since God's will is supreme in all things, when He wills or plans certain divine purposes such as the salvation of a soul or a revival in a specific area, why doesn't He arbitrarily go over our heads and carry out His will? Why did He set up a system which made Him "dependent" upon a man? Is this not a baffling mystery?

God Begs Men to Pray

That He will do nothing in the realm of human

redemption, since its inception, outside of this scheme of prayer and intercession is indicated by God's many pressing invitations to prayer in His Word. He not only invites us; He intreats, He importunes, He urges. He even begs us to exercise this privilege. One translator has paraphrased Matthew 7:7 thus: "Ask, I ask you to ask; seek, I intreat you to seek; knock, I urge you to knock." Evidently He can do nothing without our prayers.

He not only invites and exhorts us to pray, He also commands: "Pray ye therefore the Lord of the harvest, that he will send forth labourers into his harvest" (Matt. 9:38). He is Himself the Lord of the harvest. The harvest is His. The laborers are His. *Why* should He stand "helplessly" by while urging men to pray reapers into the fields? Why does He send forth laborers only in answer to the prayers of the redeemed?

God "Categorically" Promises to Answer

The fundamental importance of this scheme of prayer in God's economy is further emphasized by God's binding Himself unequivocally to answer. God's promises to answer prayer are so sweeping and "categorical," over such a broad spectrum, as to constitute a veritable carte blanche, that is, a blank card bearing the authority of His own signature. It is as though God handed us His scepter and begged us to use it. Here are some examples: "And whatsoever ye shall ask in my name, that will I do. . . . If ye shall ask anything in my name, I will do it" (John 14:13-14). "If ye abide in me, and my words abide in you, ye shall ask what ye will and it shall be done unto you" (John 15:7). "Verily, verily, I say unto you, Whatsoever ye shall ask the Father in my name, he will give it you. Hitherto have ye asked nothing in my name; ask, and ye shall receive, that your joy may be full" (John 16:23-24).

His Plan of Prayer "Watertight"

I call these categorical promises, meaning they are

unqualified or unconditional. When I use that term I mean that no conditions are attached which constitute a hedge on God's part. In other words, there are no conditions which are not fair or which are not within the reasonable capacity of a truly dedicated child of God. The condition of abiding in Him and His words abiding in us is possible for any ordinary, earnest, and sincere born-again believer. If it is not possible for such believers, then we would have to say that God is hedging, that is, seeking to avoid the risk involved in making such sweeping promises — and that is impossible for Him. But if God is not hedging, *then the entire reponsibility for prayerlessness or ineffective prayer falls entirely upon us.* And if asking in the name of the Lord Jesus is not something that any fully devoted believer can normally do, then again God is hedging. But God is not hedging. He is dealing honorably. Therefore, the responsibility for prayerlessness or unanswered prayer must fall upon us. The scheme of prayer, so far as God is concerned, is "watertight." His part is already done. While His promise to answer is always circumscribed by His will, this is in no sense a hedge since any truly yielded child of God never wills anything but God's will. In other words, there is no "fine print" in God's prayer contract.

God Proposes — A Holy Church Disposes

God's offer of His scepter to redeemed humanity is, therefore, a bona fide offer. It is an offer in good faith. Through the plan of prayer God actually is inviting redeemed man into FULL partnership with Him, not in *making* the divine decisions, but in *implementing* those decisions in the affairs of humankind. Independently and of His own will God makes the decisions governing the affairs of earth. *The responsibility and authority for the enforcement and administration of those decisions He has placed upon the shoulders of His Church.* "I say also unto thee that thou art Peter, and upon this rock I will build my church, and the gates of hell shall not prevail against it.[1] And I will give unto thee the keys of the kingdom of heaven; and whatsoever thou shall bind on earth shall be bound in heaven, and whatsoever thou shalt loose on earth shall be loosed in heaven'' (Matt. 16:18-19). This promise is repeated to the Church in general in Matthew 18:18: ''Verily I say unto you, Whatsoever ye shall bind on earth shall be bound in heaven; and whatsoever ye shall loose on earth shall be loosed in heaven.'' ''Behold, I give unto *you* power [authority] to tread on serpents and scorpions, and over all the power of the enemy; and nothing shall by any means hurt you'' (Luke 10:19). ''As my Father hath sent me, even so send I you. Whose soever sins ye remit, they are remitted unto them; and whose soever sins ye retain, they are retained'' (John 20:21-23).

God Deputizes His Church

In commenting on John 20:21-23 as a part of the Easter Sunday School lesson for April 14, 1968, Dr. Wilbur T. Dayton says, ''After the removal of His bodily presence from among them, His followers must be His representatives, must take His place. This is the apostle's commission and ours. We are His proxies with power of attorney to do His bidding.'' ''As the Father hath sent me, even so send I you'' can mean nothing less than that we are His deputies with full authority to enforce the divine will and program. The deputy is invested with the full power of the office of his Chief, and is fully authorized to act in His stead.

Why?

The question is: *Why* did God choose to work within the framework of this system of prayer? *Why* did He place the full responsibility for the enforcement and administration of the divine government of earth and its affairs upon the shoulders of fallen but redeemed humanity? *Why* will He do nothing in earthly affairs apart from the cooperation of

His Church? While we rightly reject the Roman idea that the Pope is God's vicegerent on earth, *have we not failed to act upon the sweeping authority God has delegated to His corporate body in the world?* And that authority to implement the will and decision of God concerning earthly affairs operates solely within the framework and system of prayer which God has ordained. By God's own decree, all of this vast delegated authority is wholly inoperative apart from the prayers of man (Ezekiel 20:30-31). What is the explanation of this plan? *Why* did God do it?

Prayer Privilege — The Badge of Rank

God had something infinitely great in mind when He planned the system of prayer. God's eternal purpose in the creation of the universe and the human race was to obtain an Eternal Companion for His Son. This fact is a part of the mystery revealed in the Book of Ephesians, reaching its illuminative climax in chapter five. This chapter expounds the divinely revealed parallel between God's human and divine marriage programs. Verse 32 clarifies the mystery when Paul unequivocally declares that the partners in the marriage program are Christ and His Church.[2] In God's eternal purpose the Church, as Christ's Eternal Companion, is to occupy the highest position in the universe short of the Godhead itself. As the Bride of the Eternal Son she is to share with Him universal sovereignty. "Don't you know that some day we Christians are going to judge and govern the world? . . . Don't you realize that we Christians will judge and reward the very · angels in heaven?" (1 Cor. 6:2a, 3a *LB*). "If we suffer, we shall also reign with him" (2 Tim. 2:12). "And he that overcometh, and keepeth my works unto the end, to him will I give power [authority] over the nations" (Rev. 2:26). "To him that overcometh will I grant to sit with me in my throne, even as I also overcame, and am set down with my Father in his throne" (Rev. 3:21). "And they sang a new song, saying, Thou art worthy to take the scroll, and to open its seals; for thou wast slain, and has redeemed us to God by thy blood out of every kindred, and tongue, and people, and nation; and hast made us unto our God a kingdom of priests, and we shall reign on the earth (Rev. 5:9-10 *New Scofield*). *Redeemed members of the human race, the only race in all creation that was made in the image of God, will constitute this Eternal Companion. Since this companion is to share the throne of the universe with her Lover and Lord she must be trained, educated, and prepared for her queenly role.*

Prayer Is "On-the-job" Training for Sovereignty

By delegating His authority to her for administering His decisions and enforcing His will upon earth, God placed the Church in apprenticeship for eternal sovereignty with Christ. By practicing in her prayer closet the enforcement of Heaven's decisions in mundane affairs, the Church is in "on-the-job" training for co-sovereignty with Christ over His universal empire. She must learn the art of spiritual warfare, of overcoming evil forces in preparation for her assumption of the throne following the Marriage Supper of the Lamb. *To enable her to learn the technique of overcoming, God devised the scheme of prayer. To give her "on-the-job" training, God delegated to her the authority to enforce His will right here on earth. In order to enable her to acquire the character and the "know how" she will need as co-sovereign, He has placed upon her the responsibility and authority to enforce God's will and administer His decisions in the affairs of earth.*

Notice how often *earth*, as her sphere of action, is emphasized: "Whatsoever thou shalt bind on *earth*"; "Whatsoever thou shalt loose on *earth*"; "If any two of you shall agree on *earth*." (Matt. 16:19, Matt. 18:18-19). This delegation of authority and administrative responsibility for earthly affairs constitutes the highest honor and elevates her to the highest rank of all created beings. No angel nor archangel will ever achieve this rank, because not angels but redeemed humanity alone is qualified by original creation in the image and likeness of God to constitute the Bride and share the Bridegroom's throne.

Supreme Rank — God's Original Purpose

It may seem irreverent, but it is nevertheless true, that God cannot exalt redeemed humanity any higher in the divine economy without infringing upon the Godhead. While we must understand that infinity separates the Creator from the created, yet from the beginning God planned in Jesus Christ so completely to bridge this gap that redeemed humanity ends up as a full-blooded (generic) member of the family of God, seated with Christ on the throne of the universe as His Bride and Companion. "To him that overcometh will I grant to sit with me in my throne" (Rev. 3:21). This was no afterthought. It was God's plan from all eternity. "He hath chosen us *in him* before the foundation of the world" (Eph. 1:4). *This was God's original purpose in the creation of the universe and the human race. And God's prayer program is His method of preparing the Bride for her future queenly role.*

If the Church Will Not Pray, God Will Not Act

This is why God never goes "over the head" of His Church to enforce His decisions. He will not take things out of her hands. To do so would sabotage His training program. Only by bearing this overwhelming weight of responsibility can she be brought to her full stature as co-sovereign of the universe. This is why when she fails He will wait. This is why He will do nothing in the realm of human redemption until she accepts her responsibility and uses her privilege and prerogative of intercession. If she will not pray God will not act because this would abort His purpose to bring His Church to her full potential as His co-sovereign.

This was God's plan from the beginning. He will not spoil it now by taking things out of her hands. *He will let the whole world go to destruction first.* His part of the work of redemption is full and complete. But He will not override His Church. *His eternal purpose is the qualifiying of His Eternal Companion for entering into full partnership with her Lord in the governing process of the universe.* She can be qualified only through the apprenticeship of prayer and intercession. Only thus does she learn to enter into and participate in the eternal purpose of her Lord. Therefore, *God will do nothing apart from His Church.*

Prayer — The Main Business of the Church

This is why John Wesley said, ''God will do nothing but in answer to prayer.'' This is why S. D. Gordon said that ''The greatest thing anyone can do for God and for man is to pray.'' This is why he also said, ''You can do more than pray *after* you have prayed, but you cannot do more than pray *until* you have prayed.'' This also explains his statement, ''Prayer is striking the winning blow . . . service is gathering up the results.'' It likewise explains the statement of E. M. Bounds about prayer: ''God shapes the world by prayer. The more praying there is in the world the better the world will be, the mightier the forces against evil . . . . The prayers of God's saints are the capital stock of heaven by which God carries on His great work upon earth. God conditions the very life and prosperity of His cause on prayer.'' If these things are true, then ''prayer should be the main business of our day.''

The Church Holds the Key

Checks used by some business firms require the signatures of two individuals to make them valid. One signature is not enough. Both parties must sign. This illustrates God's method of operating through the prayers and faith of His people. His promises are His checks signed in His own blood. His part was fully completed at Calvary.

But no promise is made good until a redeemed man enters the throne room of the universe and, by prayer and faith, writes his name beside God's. Then, and not until then, are the check's resources released. It is like a safety deposit box in the bank vault. The keeper has a key and you have a key. Neither key alone will open the box. But, when you give the keeper your key, she inserts *both* keys and the door flies open, making available all of the treasure stored in the box. *Heaven holds the key by which decisions governing earthly affairs are made but we hold the key by which those decisions are implemented.* This being so, then prayer takes on a very different dimension from the conventional notion or understanding. *Prayer is not overcoming reluctance in God.* It is not persuading Him to do something He is unwilling to do. It is "binding upon earth" that which already has been bound in heaven (Matt. 16:19 *Amplified*). *It is implementing His decision. It is enforcing His will upon earth.* Prayer makes possible God's accomplishing what He wants and what He cannot do without it. The content of all true prayer originates in the heart of God. So it is He who inspires the prayer in the heart of man, and the answer to every God-inspired petition is already prepared before the prayer is uttered. When we are convinced of this, then faith for the answer is easy — far easier than it would be otherwise.

Too Busy to Pray

No angel was ever invited to share this high privilege. No archangel was ever invited into the throne room of the universe. Only redeemed humanity. And many of us are too busy — watching television, following sports, hunting and fishing, bathing and boating, engaging in farming or business, moonlighting, etc., etc. We are so busy with the cares and pleasures of this life, trying to keep up with the trend in new cars, new homes, new appliances, new furniture, etc., that we do not have time to pray.

Someone has described a modern American as a person who drives a bank-financed car over a bond-financed highway on credit card gas to open a charge account at a department store so he can fill his Savings and Loan financed home with installment-purchased furniture. May this not also be a description of many modern professed Christians? And may this not be one reason why modern Christians have so little time to pray?

Perhaps some may be thinking: Are we to have nothing at all for ourselves? The answer is, NO. Christ is to be ALL and in all. You are not your own. You are bought with a price (1 Cor. 6:19-20). "Whether therefore ye eat, or drink, or whatsoever ye do, do all to the glory of God" (1 Cor. 10:31). If you can buy the new car, the new home, the new furniture, the new gadgets, hold down two jobs, etc., for the glory of God — well and good. But if we didn't have to have such a high standard of living would we not have more time to pray? If we were not so intoxicated with travel, pleasure, vacations, and recreation, would we not have more time to pray? If we were not so enamored of sports and entertainment, would we not have more time to pray? We have more leisure than ever before — but less time to pray. We are not only cheating God and the world but we are cheating ourselves. By our failure to pray we are frustrating God's high purpose in the ages. We are robbing the world of God's best plan for it and we are limiting our rank in eternity.

"AND I SOUGHT FOR A MAN AMONG THEM AND FOUND NONE."

NOTES

1.   Two similar but distinct Greek words are used in this passage: *petros,* a masculine noun translated ''Peter,'' and *petra,* a feminine noun translated ''rock.'' According to Thayer's *Greek Lexicon, petra* means ''a massive, living [unquarried] rock'' — like Gibraltar — while *petros* signifies ''a detached but large fragment.'' Here Jesus is saying He will build His Church, not upon the smaller, detached stone Peter (*petros*), but upon the huge rock (*petra*), which of course is Christ Jesus Himself. Then follows the statement that the gates of hell shall not prevail against it.

In the Orient at that time, the gate of the city was the seat of government where court was convened and where decisions were made. This is the place where counsel was held and where strategy and plans for action were devised. Thus Jesus is saying that all of the strategy and plans for attack that hell would make or invent against His Church will fail.

To a superficial observer, this sounds like a vain hope because it seems that Satan is actually succeeding in defeating God's kingdom. If the contest between God and Satan were for the loyalty of the majority of the race, then clearly Satan is the winner. But if God's real purpose is the calling out of a select group called the Church, who are being prepared and qualified for rulership in His eternal and universal kingdom, then as long as Christ is successfully obtaining and training His Church, the gates of hell are not prevailing. If Satan could succeed in preventing the calling out of the Church, then the gates of hell would prevail against it. But from the birth of the Church to this present throbbing moment Satan has never been able to stop the calling out of the Church. Through opposition, persecution, and martyrdom the Church has marched on. Neither suffering nor affliction nor tribulation; neither calamity, distress, persecution nor hunger; neither destitution nor peril nor fire nor sword; none of these have availed to stop the onward march of the Church. Therefore, the gates of hell have *not* prevailed against the Church.

2.   The mystery of God's celestial marriage program is heightened by the concept of a "multiple" bride. To many this seems inappropriate because in earthly marriage we think of a bride in the singular. This difficulty vanishes when we adopt Paul's concept of the Church as an organic body. "For as the body is one, and hath many members, and all the members of that one body, being many, are one body, so also is Christ. . . .For the body is not one member but many" (1 Cor. 12:12,14).

We consider the human body as a single entity because it is united by a single consciousness. Yet Paul emphasizes that it is not one, but many members. Just so, the Holy City of John's vision, which constitutes the heavenly Bride, is inhabited not by one but by an immense multitude. Yet because it will be united by a single consciousness it will compose a single, harmonious whole comparable to the unity of the human body. This is the unity toward which the Church is moving in time and which will be realized in absolute perfection by the bridehood inhabitants of the heavenly city, the New Jerusalem, which John saw descending out of heaven from God. That city will be inhabited by an innumerable throng so perfectly fused into one consciousness by holy passion for the heavenly Bridegroom, that it will constitute a single organism. Can this be why God prizes unity among His people so highly and why Satan fights it so desperately?

4

CHRIST'S GIFT OF AUTHORITY

Behold, I give unto you power to tread on serpents and scorpions, and over all the power of the enemy; and nothing shall by any means hurt you (Luke 10:19).

The Church's Magna Carta

Following the return of the seventy and their jubilant report that even the demons were subject unto them, Jesus replies with a most amazing and startling statement, the significance of which apparently has escaped many believers. He first announced that he had personally witnessed Satan's expulsion from heaven. It was *His* word of authority that cast him forth so that Satan as lightning fell from heaven (Luke 10:18). *Now* He places in *their* hands that same word of authority. Now He is saying, "I hand this authority over to *you*." "Behold, I give unto *you* power to tread on serpents [evil spirits] and scorpions [demons] and over *all* the power of the enemy [Satan]; and nothing shall by any means hurt you" (Luke 10:19, Heb. 2:14-15).

This is the Church's Magna Carta in her conflict with Satan. Here is a clear *legal* basis for deliverance from Satan's bondage and oppression, and for offensive action in the conflict with him. *It is clear from this and other passages that God intends the true Church, not Satan, to be the controlling factor in human affairs.*

Organic Unity

In Ephesians 1:20-22 Paul explains that Christ is the supreme authority in the universe, exalted far above every other name or power or governing authority in creation, and that all things in heaven and on earth have been placed under His feet, that is, under His absolute dominion. Then Paul adds that He is the Head of the Church which is His body. Here is not only functional but organic relationship. This is not a mystical, philosophical, symbolic, allegorical or institutional relationship but *organic unity*. To illustrate: the members of a board of directors of a corporation have only functional relationship to one another. But an arm or hand or foot has an organic relationship to the body because each member draws its life from the life of the body. Just so, the born-again believer has an organic relationship to Christ because his source of life is in Him. The Church is not merely an institution ruled over by Christ as President, a kingdom in which He is the supreme authority, but an organism which is in vital connection with Him, having the source of its life in Him.

Organic Unity Prefigured

This organic relationship is foreshadowed or prefigured in the creation of a bride for the first Adam. Among all the lower orders of life there was found no fit companion for him (Gen. 2:20). None of them partook of his nature. So Adam was sent into a "deep sleep" and from a wound in his side a portion of his own body was taken and a helper suitable for him was made. "Now there was a being in life who could understand Adam, one who could enter into his plans, ideals, aims, hopes and fears, one who could love as he loved and live as he lived in a manner such as none of the lower orders could" (T. H. Nelson). "And Adam said, This is now bone of my bones, and flesh of my flesh" (Gen. 2:23). This was *organic* relationship.

In 1 Corinthians 15:44-47 Christ is called the "second man," the "last Adam." As the antitype of the first Adam it was necessary that Christ, the second Man or Last Adam, also have a bride. Like the first Adam, He too went into a "deep sleep," of death and resurrection. Out of his wounded side the Church, through faith, is born of God as the Bride of Christ. In Revelation 21:9 she is called the Bride, the Lamb's Wife, and in Ephesians 5, the chapter dealing with both earthly and heavenly nuptials, Paul reveals in verse 30 that as Eve was of Adam so we, the Church, are "members of his body, of his flesh, and of his bones." The Church is His Body now. She will be His Bride at the Marriage Supper of the Lamb.

On the Throne Because of Organic Unity

All of the foregoing clearly supports the organic character of the unity between Christ and His Church. If Christ has been exalted as the Supreme Authority in the universe and is now seated at the right hand of the Father wielding all of the authority of the Godhead, both in heaven and on earth; and if the Church as His Body is organically united with Him as the Head, where does that place the Church? Can it be elsewhere except upon the throne with Christ? And this agrees with Paul's statement of the fact in Ephesians 2:5-6 where he says that after making us alive with Christ, God raised us up together with Him and seated us together in heavenly places in Christ Jesus. In other words, we have already been legally enthroned with Christ because we are organically united with Him and have, therefore, already here and now entered upon our reign with Him. We are co-crucified, co-raised, co-exalted, co-seated with Christ.[1]

Practical Effects of Organic Unity

Although to the natural mind this seems utter nonsense, it is nevertheless true. In spite of all her lamentable weaknesses, appalling failures and indefensible shortcomings, the Church is the mightiest force for civilization and enlightened social consciousness in the world today. It was true in the ancient world that as the knowledge of and reverence for God disappeared, moral corruption and crime completly destroyed the social order. ''The earth also was corrupt before God, and the earth was filled with violence. And God looked upon the earth, and, behold, it was corrupt; for all flesh had corrupted his way upon the earth. And God said unto Noah, The end of all flesh is come before me; for the earth is filled with violence through them; and, behold, I will destroy them with the earth'' (Gen. 6:11-13). It is the same today. The only force in the world that is contesting Satan's total rule in human affairs is the Church of the living God. If Satan were unopposed, if he were under no restraint because of the Spirit-inspired prayers and holy lives of God's people, ''the pillared firmament itself were rottenness and earth's base built on stubble.'' If there were nothing to hinder him, Satan would make a hell out of this world here and now. The only saving and healing virtue in the howling deserts of human life flows from the cross of Calvary. The only pure unselfishness in the world issues from the fountain filled with blood. If it were not for the totally selfless love displayed on the bloody cross, total selfishness would reign supreme. And total selfishness means total hostility. Total hostility means total anarchy — *and that means hell.*

Civilization a By-Product of the Gospel

All the blessings of peace and tranquility, without which there can be no stable social order and no civilization as we know it, are the result of the gospel. And the true Church is the custodian of that gospel. Therefore, the true Church is not only the central and fundamental but also the vital institution upon which every other structure — social, political, and governmental — depends. Without the moral and spiritual light shed abroad by the Word of God through the Church, there would be no favorable climate for business and commerce or enlightening cultural, educational, and social activities. Without the knowledge of and reverence for God, there can be no orderly and efficient functioning of government. All of the processes of democracy and civilization as we know them require an umbrella of law and order under which to function. This umbrella is maintained and supported effectively only where the gospel has spread its benign and life-giving influence. What we know as Western civilization, providing the highest standard of living, the greatest freedom and personal security, the most domestic peace and tranquility the world has ever known, is definitely a by-product of the Judeo-Christian ethic and the redemption wrought by Jesus Christ.

The Church Wields the Balance of Power

From the womb of the gospel, then, are born all the principles, standards, and qualities of character which form the foundation of all moral, spiritual, social, and political well-being. The Church is the trustee and steward of that gospel. To the extent to which the Church has been faithful to that trust, to that extent she historically has been the saving and preserving influence in human affairs. To the extent that the Church has been faithful to her trust, to that extent she has been the basic benevolent factor in the world. To the extent that the Church has been faithful to her trust, to that extent she has wielded the balance of power in overcoming disintegration and decay in the cosmic order.

Jesus was not speaking in fables and fairy tales when He said to His disciples in Matthew 5:13, 14: "Ye are the salt of the earth"; "Ye are the light of the world." The world at large is totally blind to this fact, but if it were not for the purifying and preserving influence of the Church the fabric of all we call civilization would totally disintegrate, decay, and disappear. At this present throbbing moment the Church, in union with her risen and enthroned Lord is, therefore, the fundamental preserving factor in this present world order. *Therefore, by virtue of her organic relationship with Christ, the Supreme Sovereign, she, not Satan, holds the balance of power in human affairs.* It has been truly said, *"The fate of the world is in the hands of nameless saints."* This truth is wonderfully set forth in Psalm 149:5-9: "Let the saints be joyful in glory; let them sing aloud upon their beds. Let the high praises of God be in their mouth, and a twoedged sword in their hand, to execute vengeance upon the heathen, and punishments upon the people; to bind their kings with chains, and their nobles with fetters of iron; to execute upon them the judgment written. *This honour have all his saints.* Praise ye the Lord."

If it were not for the Church, Satan would already have turned this earth into hell. The fact that it has been preserved from total devastation in spite of him, proves that at least a remnant of the Church is effectually functioning and already has entered upon her rulership in union with her Lord. She is even now, by virtue of the scheme of prayer and faith, engaged in "on-the-job" training for her place as co-sovereign with Christ over the entire universe following Satan's final destruction.

George Washington, the Father of our Country, recognized the validity of these principles when he said, "It is impossible rightly to govern the world without God and the Bible." And that prince of statesmen, Daniel Webster, said, "If we abide by the principles taught in the Bible, our country will go on prospering and to prosper; but if we or our posterity neglect its instructions and authority, no man can tell how sudden a catastrophe may overwhelm us and bury all our glory in profound obscurity." In the light of the present dissolution of our existing social and political institutions, these words seem amazingly prophetic.

The Church's Authority and Free Will [2]

The validity of these principles in world affairs at large is fairly well documented. But are these principles applicable in personal and individual cases? In the instance of the salvation of a specific individual, who holds the balance of power, Satan or the Church? Does the authority which God has offered the Church reach into the domain of free moral agency?[3] Is this delegated authority compatible with free will? God has said in His Word that He wills that all men be saved. Knowing that it is God's will to save any man who has not crossed that mysterious boundary known as the deadline, may the Church pray for the salvation of a specific individual in the assurance that he will be saved? Or, must the Church's faith be tempered by the fact that that person is a free moral agent and that God never saves any man against his will? *Must* we say, as we so often do, that because "so and so" is a free moral agent, all we can do is to pray and leave the rest to him and God? Since God has assured us that it is His will that all men be saved, we therefore know that when we pray for the salvation of anyone who has not crossed the deadline of final and permanent impenitence, we are praying according to His will. In 1 John 5:14-15 the apostle says, "And this is the confidence we have in him, that, if we ask any thing according to his will, he heareth us; and if we know that he hear us, whatsoever we ask, we know that we have the petitions that we desired of him." Now the question is: Is this promise neutralized by the free moral agency of man? Do we have to stand back and watch Satan capture a soul because God does not save anyone against his will? Is it correct to say that all we can do is to pray and leave the rest to God and the individual?

Were Not All of Us Rebels?

May I answer that question by asking another? *Do you*

believe that anyone was ever saved who was not, in the beginning, a rebel? Were not all of us born with our backs against God? Did we not all, like Adam, run and hide from God? Did we not all mightily resist the wooing of God's Spirit before we were saved? And did we not all continue to resist that wooing until it became so persuasive and compelling that it finally became easier to yield than to continue in that rebellion? Did there not come a point when rebellion crossed over into surrender, not because the will was coerced, but because it was more painful to resist than to yield? And although the will yielded it could have, if it had chosen, continued in rebellion.

The Determining Factor in Salvation

Is not this the general pattern of the journey from rebellion to surrender? Jesus says, "No man can come to me except the Father . . . draw him" (John 6:44). And the Father always draws by means of His Spirit. Since God is no respecter of persons and wills that all shall be saved, and therefore without exception faithfully seeks all (John 1:9), *why* is the Spirit's wooing successful in some cases and not in others? Is it because in some instances God is so "powerless" that He cannot prevail? *Or* is it that some are the subjects of powerful, importunate, and believing intercession while others have no one to pray for them? If Wesley is correct in saying that "God does nothing but in answer to prayer," then this must include the salvation of souls. *This, then, means that no soul is saved apart from intercession, and that every soul who is saved, is saved because someone prayed who would not give him up to Satan.* We agree that God desires all men to be saved. He has made provision for the salvation of all. "Behold the Lamb of God, which taketh away the sin of the world" (John 1:29). "And he is the propitiation for our sins, and not for ours only, but also for the sins of the *whole world*" (1 John 2:2). Although it is God's will that all be saved, and although He has made provision for the salvation of the whole world, *this salvation is limited wholly and entirely by the intercession, or lack of it, of the Church. Those for whom the Church travails are saved. All others are lost.*

"And when he had said this, he breathed on them, and saith unto them, Receive ye the Holy Ghost; whose soever sins ye remit, they are remitted unto them; and whose soever sins ye retain, they are retained" (John 20:22-23).[4]

The Spirit and the Bride

The Holy Spirit has the power to so enlighten the mind, awaken the spirit, and move the emotions of a man that he will find it easier to yield than to continue his rebellion. *God will not go over the head of His Church even to save a soul without her cooperation. If she will not intercede, the Holy Spirit, by His own choice, cannot do His office work of convicting and persuading.* By virtue of His purpose to qualify His Bride for her eternal rulership with Him, He has chosen to save no soul until she travails. "The Spirit *and* the bride say, Come" (Rev. 22:17). Not the Spirit alone, but the Spirit *and* the Bride. *He will do nothing without her.* Hence He *can* do nothing without her. [5]

If she does not travail, the Spirit does not woo. If the Spirit does not woo, the soul is lost. But the Spirit can and will woo; He can and will persuade any soul who has not crossed the deadline, for whom the Church travails.

The Power of Life or Death

This being so, then the Church, not Satan, holds the balance of power not only in world affairs but in the salvation of individual souls. *Therefore a holy Church, by her intercession or lack of it, holds the power of life or death over the souls of men.* Without violating a person's free moral agency (full moral responsibility), the Spirit can so powerfully persuade that soul that he will voluntarily yield. But He does this only in answer to believing prayer and intercession of a believing Church. May this not be why some are powerfully convicted and converted while others are lost?

The Damascus Road Experience

The conversion of the apostle Paul is pertinent to this point. We are not told specifically that the Church was praying for Saul, its most deadly foe, but can anyone doubt that they were, just as they did in the case of Peter in prison when ''prayer was made without ceasing of the church unto God for him'' (Acts 12:5)? It can hardly be doubted that desperate intercession was made for him, since the very life of the Church was at stake. And can it be doubted that the intercession of these early believers made possible the Damascus Road confrontation that completely revolutionized Christ's worst human enemy and tranformed him into His great apostle? The apostle's will was not coerced. He was convinced and persuaded and chose to yield. If God, in answer to the prayers of the Church, could so reveal Himself to Paul as to cause him to voluntarily embrace the Christ he had so fiercely hated and persecuted, is *anyone* beyond the reach of God's Spirit when the Church likewise travails?

Paul's Mighty Weapons

Perhaps you are not yet convinced that these principles extend to the domain of free moral agency or full moral responsibility. Perhaps you doubt that the authority of the Church is valid in personal and individual cases, because of the free will of man. Perhaps you still feel that where the salvation of a specific individual is concerned, all we can do is to pray and leave the rest to him and God. May I refer all such to the words of the apostle Paul in 2 Corinthians 10:4-5: ''I use God's mighty weapons, not those made by man, to knock down the devil's strongholds. These weapons can break down every proud argument against God and every wall that can be built to keep men from finding him. *With these weapons I can capture rebels and bring them back to God, and change them into men whose hearts' desire is obedience to Christ''* (LB).[6]

Freedom of Choice

Was Paul ignoring the free moral agency or full moral responsibility of men when he wrote these words? Or was he thinking of the way the Holy Spirit struck him down on the Damascus road that day, even while he was breathing out threatenings and slaughter against Christ and His followers? Was he remembering what the Celestial Voice said about the pain of kicking against the goad? Was he thinking about how his own heart's desire was instantly changed by the powerful illumination of the Holy Spirit into a desire to obey Christ? Was this the inspiration for his faith that these same weapons, which changed him from a rebel into a willing ''captive'' of Christ, were just as effective in his hands ''to capture rebels and bring them back to God''?

Notice that in the use of these weapons Paul does not violate the freedom of choice of the rebels. He does not use coercion. By means of these weapons he changes them from rebellion to voluntary cooperation. Their free will is not violated. They become willing ''captives'' of Christ. If such weapons were available to Paul are they not also available to the Church to whom Christ gave authority over all the power of the enemy?

A Rebel Won

My mother used these weapons on me. I was as hostile to God as any sinner. I was fighting with all my might. But the time came when it was easier to lay down my arms of rebellion than to continue my resistance. The pressure exerted upon me by the Holy Spirit became so powerful that I voluntarily sought relief by yielding my rebellious will. The wooing of divine love was so strong that of my own free will I fell into the arms of redeeming grace. I became a willing ''captive.''

God can and does deal thus with any sinner when the Church learns to use these mighty weapons of importunate prayer and faith. It is my firm belief that wherever a soul has not crossed the deadline, a believing Church may pray in full assurance and faith for that soul's salvation. Hallelujah!

"FOR AS SOON AS ZION TRAVAILED, SHE BROUGHT FORTH HER CHILDREN" (Isa. 66:8).

NOTES

1.   To many people this constitutes an impossible enigma, an incomprehensible riddle, an impenetrable mystery. How can we be organically united with Christ and seated with Him in the heavens when our feet are pressing "terra firma" and we are engaged in the prosaic occupations of daily life? Paul gives us the key to this mystery in 1 Corinthians 6:17: "He that is joined to the Lord is one spirit." In some philosophical systems, spirit is considered to be "essential reality." Material is said to be accidental; that is, it derives its reality from its relationship to spirit. For instance, when the spirit leaves the body, the body disintegrates. It loses its structure because it is dependent upon the spirit for its organization as reality. The spirit has independent reality. The body has only relative reality. It is the spirit that gives life to and sustains the body. This is what we mean when we say that the spirit is essential reality and that material is only accidental, or has only relative reality. In other words, your spirit is the real "you," the real person. *Therefore, a person who is joined to the Lord as one spirit is, in his essential being, seated with Christ in the heavens.* While the body is here, the real self is there. While a body may occupy only one place at a time, spirit is not so confined. Because "he that is joined to the Lord is one spirit," therefore, since Christ is exalted and enthroned, the Church is exalted and enthroned with Him.

2.   Nothing in this or the following paragraphs should be construed as releasing the sinner from full responsibility for his own salvation. The Church's responsibility ends with faithfulness in intercession. Only the Holy Spirit knows when that point is reached. The sinner is totally responsible. The Church's responsibility is bounded by the principle of free moral agency.

3.   The term "free moral agency" is not here used in its absolute sense, since God alone is absolutely "free." But although man's will

has been warped by the fall, he is still responsible for his decisions.

4.   Controversy has surrounded the interpretation of John 20:23: "Whose soever sins ye remit, they are remitted unto them; and whose soever sins ye retain, they are retained." It almost shocks us that Christ has delegated authority for the forgiveness of sins to the disciples and hence to the Church. But in a very real sense this is true. By exercising her God-given authority of prayer and faith, the Church opens the way for the Holy Spirit to do His office work of conviction and persuasion. Through the work of the Spirit, in answer to the believing prayer of the true Church or members thereof, the sinner is brought to the place of voluntary repentance and faith for forgiveness. And God, the one who alone has power to forgive sin, does the actual absolution. However, since this takes place only as the result of the Church's travail, she is in truth involved in the absolution. Therefore Jesus could say to the disciples and hence to a holy Church, "whose soever sins ye remit, they are remitted; and whose soever sins ye retain they are retained." In a very real sense, then, the responsibility for absolution is in the hands of a travailing Church, rather than a priest who may claim this authority.

5.   In the Old Testament, Israel was considered as the wife of Jehovah. Although the Marriage Supper of the Lamb has not been celebrated, since spiritually the Church is the new Israel, it does not seem inappropriate to think of the church as having inherited this wifely relationship. "Wherefore, my brethren, ye also are become dead to the law by the body of Christ, that ye should be married to another, even to him who is raised from the dead, that we should bring forth fruit unto God" (Rom. 7:4). The bringing of a new life into the human family involves the agreement and cooperation of two persons: the loving father and the pure, unselfish mother. And that life does not come into the world without travail. Reflecting this analogy, the divine spirit Father and the pure Church mother must agree and cooperate in bringing newborn souls into the family of God. And neither can these be born without travail. *There is no easy soul-winning.* And the work of the Spirit is ineffective without the cooperation of the travailing Church. By His own choice, the Spirit alone cannot bring a soul to birth. The cooperation of both is necessary. The Church's part as intercessor is just as necessary as the Spirit's part. "The Spirit *and* the bride say, Come."

6.   It is recognized that the accuracy of the paraphrase is pertinent.

5

THE LEGAL BASIS OF THE AUTHORITY OF THE CHURCH

Was Calvary a Victory or a Defeat?

It is vitally important for every believer to know with absolute certainty that Calvary was an unutterably glorious triumph. Unless the believer fully understands and is immutably convinced of the infallible basis of his faith, he will be hampered by misgivings and will be unable effectually to exercise his authority over Satan. This and the following chapter are designed to remove any such doubt and to show that Christ, through Calvary and the descent into hell, totally and irrevocably defeated and disarmed Satan both legally and dynamically, so that Paul refers to the satanic forces as "the dethroned powers that rule" (1 Cor. 2:6 *Moffatt*).

The reality of Christ's victory at Calvary is being openly challenged today by the new and growing church of Satanism. Calvary is being represented by them as a defeat, a stupid display of supine weakness.

According to *The Satanic Bible*, the crucifix symbolizes "pallid incompetence hanging on a tree." In *The Satanic Rituals* Satan is called "the ineffable Prince of Darkness who rules the earth." He is further envisioned as seizing the initiative from Christ, who is called "the lasting foulness of Bethlehem," "the cursed Nazarene," "impotent king," "fugitive and mute god," "vile and abhorred pretender to the majesty of Satan.''

Satan is described as ''great Satan,'' ''Prince of Darkness,'' ''Satan — Lucifer who rules the earth,'' who will send the ''Christian minions staggering to their doom.'' He is also depicted as ''the Lord of Light'' — with Christ's angels, cherubim, and seraphim ''cowering and trembling with fear'' and ''prostrating themselves before him'' while he ''sends the gates of heaven crashing down.''

This is an example of the way Satan constantly seeks to persuade the Church and the world that he is almost, if not quite, as powerful as God. The world is fairly well convinced by this pretense, and the Church herself suffers under its pressure. This is because Satan has successfully concealed from the Church what actually happened to him, not only at Calvary, but also between Calvary and the resurrection. To the world at large and to many believers, Calvary appears as a defeat. In spite of our professed faith, many of us are hounded with the sneaking suspicion that Satan was, after all, the victor there. An examination of the forensic aspects (legal phases) of the conflict between Christ and Satan proves conclusively the triumph of the Crucified. The legal aspect of that victory is the theme of this chapter.

Adam's Commission: Dominion Over the Earth

In order to understand what happened at Calvary, one must first comprehend what took place legally in the fall in Eden. Man was originally made for authority. He was created and fashioned for dominion. When he came from the hand of God he was given the rulership of the earth, the kingship of its life, and the control and mastery of its resources. In Genesis 1:26 it is recorded, ''And God said, Let us make man in our image, after our likeness; and let them have dominion over the fish of the sea, and over the fowl of the air, and over the cattle, and over all the earth, and over every creeping thing that creepeth upon the earth.'' The writer of the eighth Psalm adds this comment: ''Thou madest him to have dominion over the works of thy hands; thou hast put all things under his feet.''

Adam's Tragic Failure

The entire universe is governed by law. Redemption from beginnning to end is based upon a system of divine jurisprudence. It has a legal foundation. God's grant of authority and dominion over the earth to man was a *bona fide* gift. This authority and dominion became *legally* his. What he did with it was his own responsibility. If, so to speak, he ''fumbled the ball'' and lost it, God could not lawfully step in and repossess it for him. Without doubt, Omnipotence had the power to void Satan's conquest of Adam and his heritage, but this would have violated His own moral principles of government. If God had gone over man's head and had forcibly repossessed the title to the earth from Satan, that would have been without due process of law.

The Search for a Legal Challenger

When Adam chose to obey Satan, he became Satan's slave. ''Know ye not that to whom ye yield yourselves servants [slaves] to obey, his servants [slaves] ye are?'' (Rom. 6:16). As a slave of Satan, Adam lost all of his legal rights, not only to his person but also to his domain. This gave Satan legal authority to rule over man and the earth. If Satan's dominion was to be revoked, a way had to be found to redeem fallen man and recover his lost authority without violating universal principles of justice. Since Satan was now the legitimate possessor of Adam and the legal ruler of the earth, God had no moral right, under His code of justice, to arbitrarily annul it. No angel could enter the contest because these legal rights were never his. Thus a member of Adam's race had to be found who could qualify to enter suit in universal court and wrest Adam's lost heritage and dominion from Satan. The government of the earth had been given to man. It was lost by man. It could be legally recovered only by a man. But where was the man who could do this? Since Adam was Satan's slave and all his progeny had endorsed Adam's rebellion, they were likewise Satan's slaves. A slave has no legal standing and cannot enter court or lawfully participate in litigation. Thus a member of the human race had to be found upon whom Satan had no claim, one who had *not* endorsed Adam's rebellion, one who could qualify to bring suit to cancel Satan's legal jurisdiction over mankind and the earth

The Problem Solved: The Incarnation

To the human mind the situation was hopeless, but *God found a way.* "When the fulness of the time was come, God sent forth his Son, made of a woman, made under the law, to redeem them that were under the law, that we might receive the adoption of sons" (Gal. 4:4). *God solved the problem by the Incarnation.* Since Jesus was conceived by the Holy Spirit, the divine nature was present in Him. Because He was sinless, Satan had no claim upon Him. But because He was "made of a woman," He was an authentic human being and could therefore qualify as a bona-fide member of the human race to enter the legal fight to reclaim Adam's lost estate.

The Necessity of the Virgin Birth

There are those who say that it makes no difference whether Jesus was divine or not. They say that nothing can ever change the life that He lived or the truth that He taught or His contribution to the world. But this is either malice aforethought or inexcusably loose logic. If Jesus was the son of Joseph and Mary, or the son of Mary and someone else, as some critics have blasphemously suggested, He would have been merely Adam's descendant. If He had sinned, He would thus have been disqualified for challenging Satan in court. A man had to be found who was authentically human but who was unquestionably divine, to become a legally recognized plaintiff. *Hence the necessity of the Virgin Birth* (Luke 1:35).

The Necessity of Moral Perfection

There is another reason why the Virgin Birth is essential. A successful challenger of Satan had to be not only an authentic member of the human race, but in addition one who, under testing, would prove to be morally and spiritually perfect. In order to furnish Satan no claim upon him, he had to live an absolutely sinless life. If Jesus were not the Son of God by Mary *by virtue of a supernatural conception,* then He was merely the son of Adam. Since only God could redeem man, Jesus had to be divine as well as human—truly the God-man. If He had not lived a sinless life, He would have come under Satan's control and would have been morally disqualified to enter this legal conflict. *In order to qualify legally, He had to be truly human. In order to qualify morally, He had to be unquestionably divine.*

Jesus, as a Man, Confronting Satan

Jesus came as an authentic member of the human race. Since He was cenceived by the Holy Spirit and virgin born, Satan had no legal claim upon Him. In order to establish a legal basis for authority over Him, it remained for Satan to attempt to induce some moral flaw or imperfection in His character or conduct. There was only one way to do this. Satan must persuade or compel Him to break fellowship or unity with His Father, to pressure Jesus to rebel and act independently. This was Satan's strategy and master plan. *This was the crux of the struggle between Jesus and the archfiend of darkness.* All the destiny of the world and the human race hung upon the outcome of this struggle. If Satan could by any means at his command prevail upon Jesus to have just one thought out of harmony with His heavenly Father, he would be victor and would remain the undisputed ruler of the world and the human race. If he could seduce the Last Adam as he did the first Adam, his rulership over the world and mankind would be forever secure.

Although Jesus was "very God of very God," He had to fight this battle and overcome as "very man of very man." It would have been contrary to universal justice and would have been a hollow victory for the Last Adam to employ weapons or use resources in this conflict which were not available to the first Adam in Eden. Although Jesus had all the resources of Divinity at His command, *He engaged Satan in this decisive contest purely as unfallen Man.*

The Struggle of the Ages

From Bethlehem to Calvary the conflict raged. In the effort to recover the lost inheritance of the first Adam, the Last Adam and the fallen "son of the morning" were locked in mortal combat. Through thirty-three years the struggle continued in undiminished fury. The fallen Lucifer, once the Light Bearer, the guardian of the throne of God, the highest of all pre-Adamic created beings, marshaled all of the available resources of the underworld in an effort to break down the allegiance of the God-man to His heavenly Father. One weakness revealed, one thought of rebellion or self will entertained, and all of Jesus' efforts to repossess the world and its enslaved race from the usurping god of this world would be lost. That foul fiend, that perverted prince of darkness, did his utmost throughout the Nazareth years, during the Temptation in the wilderness, in the opposition of the scribes and Pharisees to His ministry, in the Garden of Gethsemane, in Pilate's judgment hall, and finally in the crisis of Calvary, to force a breakdown in Jesus' allegiance to His Father and a transfer of that allegiance to Satan.

The Wilderness Temptation

In the wilderness, Satan offered Jesus a shortcut to world dominion if He would only fall down and worship him — just once. Satan alleged that authority over all the kingdoms of the world had been delivered unto him and that he gave it to whomsoever he chose. Jesus did not challenge this claim, for He knew Satan's legal basis for it. He also knew that the only way that He could redeem and recover man's lost estate was by way of Calvary. He overcame this temptation by using the Word of God, *the same Word that was and is available to Adam and all his progeny.* While Adam of course did not have the written Word, he did have the spoken Word communicated to him in the garden by the second Person of the Trinity, the preincarnate Eternal Word.

Gethsemane

The battle which continued through His ministry reached an incredible intensity in the Garden. The demonic and satanic pressure upon His spirit was so unutterably devastating that it brought Jesus to the very brink of death. He cried, "My soul is exceeding sorrowful, even unto death" (Matt. 26:38), while from His tortured face the blood drops oozed and spattered onto the ground. The mind staggers and human language bankrupts itself in attempting to describe this scene. As God, He could have called a multitude of angels to His aid, but had He done so He would not have suffered only as a man.

The Substance of the Agony

It was not the prospect of physical suffering which brought the agony in the Garden. That was nothing compared to the torture of His spirit. It was the anguish of a pure soul who knew no sin, facing the injustice of being "made sin" (2 Cor. 5:21), of being so completely identified with sin as not only to forfeit the fellowship of His Father, but to become *the object of the Father's loathing.* This was no mere legal imputation of sin. HE WAS MADE SIN. *He became the very essence of sin by dying as a sin offering.* He suffered the pollution of sin as if He had actually run the entire gamut of human transgression. He was adjudged guilty of the cumulative sin of mankind, and condemned to pay the full price and completely satisfy the demands of justice against the combined sin of the world.

The temptation of Gethsemane was to refuse to drink the "cup." The decision He had to make was whether He would retain the fellowship which He had with the Father before the world began or whether He would accept this unjust, yet genuine identification with sin. It was no fictitious temptation. This was what caused His soul to be "exceeding sorrowful, even unto death." His unspeakable agony is reflected in the bloody sweat and in His prayer, "O my Father, if it be possible, let this cup pass from me; *nevertheless,* not as I will, but as thou wilt" (Matt. 26:39). It seems that here the peak of His agony was reached. If ever there was any doubt as to the outcome, it faded after this. "Nevertheless" — upon that word hung the fate of the entire world. With that decision the crisis passed. He had accepted the "cup." After Gethsemane, what followed was almost anticlimactic. The judgment hall with its scourging and crown of thorns, the tortuous "Via Dolorosa" leading to Golgotha, the actual crucifixion; these were like the calm following the storm, until the actual moment of forsaking. In that one moment — as the hounds of hell were baying for His blood, and as the Father hid His face — the heart that could endure no more was broken, and He bowed His head and died.

Satan Vanquished by Death

In his effort to compel Jesus to rebel against His heavenly Father and transfer His allegiance to himself, Satan pushed Jesus clear up to death, "even the death of the cross." When at last Jesus bowed His head in mortal agony and dismissed His spirit without once failing in His submission to His heavenly Father, Satan was vanquished. Since Satan's great purpose in all that he did was to produce one small thought of rebellion against the Father, when Jesus died without yielding to that pressure, He conquered, although He died in doing so.

When the results of Calvary are adequately appraised, it appears for what it is: THE TRIUMPH OF THE AGES. When Jesus died without failing in the smallest detail, His death resulted not only in defeating Satan's purpose to obtain a claim upon Him — it also canceled all of Satan's legal claims upon the earth and the whole human race. Under universal jurisprudence, when a man commits murder he becomes subject to the death penalty. A convicted murderer forfeits his own life. He destroys himself. When Satan secured the death of Jesus he became, for the first time in his age-long history, a *murderer*.[1] He who had "the power of death" had slain his millions with impunity since the fall of Adam because he had a legal right to do so. As a slave-owner, Satan had legal title to Adam and all of his offspring. He could do with them what he chose. But he "who had the power of death" and had exercised it on countless millions with full immunity now committed the most colossal blunder of all his diabolical career. In his desperate effort to break Jesus' oneness with His Father he slew an innocent Man upon whom he had no legal claim. In so doing he committed murder and, in the court of divine justice, he brought upon himself the sentence of death. This illuminates and authenticates the meaning of Hebrews 2:14: "Forasmuch, then, as the children are partakers of flesh and blood, he also himself likewise took part of the same, *that through [his own] death he might destroy [render powerless] him that had the power of death, that is, the devil.*" If this means anything, it means that Satan is now "destroyed" (not annihilated, but destroyed); that all of his legal claims upon the earth and man are completely canceled. A person under final sentence of death has no legal rights whatever. *Therefore, since Calvary, Satan has absolutely no rights or claims upon anyone or anything. Whatever authority he carried with him on his banishment from heaven passed into the hands of the new Man along with the lost heritage of Adam which was restored by the TRIUMPH OF THE CRUCIFIED. HALLELUJAH!*

NOTES

1. This does not conflict with John 8:44. We read in 1 John 3:15 that "Whosoever hateth his brother is a murderer." In this sense Satan was a murderer from the beginning, but in a legal sense he became a murderer only when he slew Jesus.

6

CHRIST'S DYNAMIC VICTORY

Christ's Descent Into Hell

Christ's victory was not only legal, it was dynamic; that is, it was won by the application of irresistible force. Because He was "made sin" (2 Cor. 5:21), impregnated with sin, and became the very essence of sin, on the cross He was banished from God's presence as a loathsome thing. He and sin were made synonymous. In order to become a valid substitute He was compelled to satisfy the claims of justice by Himself alone, against the cumulative sin of the whole world, as if He were actually guilty of the sum total of that sin. His soul was made an offering for sin, the sin of all the generations of mankind (Isa. 53:10). *Eternal justice could not survive if it merely ignored the sins of the race.* That would make it a farce. Justice demanded that the full penalty for every sin of all mankind be paid by someone. This meant that it was not sufficient for Christ to offer up only His physical life on the cross.[1] *His pure human spirit had to "descend into hell"* (Eph. 4:9 and Acts 2:27). He was an authentic man with body, soul, and spirit. His spirit must not only descend into hell, but into the lowest hell. *The extreme penalty had to be paid. He must "taste death for every man"* (Heb. 2:9). *There could be no adequate substitution unless Christ actually paid, once and for all, the eternal consequences of the aggregate sin of the world.* That means that He endured all that combined humanity could suffer. T.H. Nelson said, ''If Christ in spirit did not thus 'descend into hell,' then we have no legal ground of assurance that we may escape that horrid prison.'' The Father turned Him over, not only to the agony and death of Calvary, but to the satanic torturers of His pure spirit as part of the just desert of the sin of all the race. As long as Christ was ''the essence of sin'' he was at Satan's mercy in that place of torment where all finally impenitent sinners are imprisoned upon leaving this life (Luke 16:19-31), which seems to be the headquarters from which Satan operates (Rev. 9:1,2,11). While Christ was identified with sin, Satan and the hosts of hell ruled over Him as over any lost sinner. During that seemingly endless age in the nether abyss of death, Satan did with Him as he would, and all hell was ''in carnival.'' This is part of what Jesus bore for us.

The Agonies of Divine Justice

The agonies which Christ endured in that dark prison are believed to be described in Psalm 88: ''He [the Father] laid him in the lowest pit, the pit of the underworld, in the dark place, in dense darkness. I [Jesus] am full of trouble, weighted with evils. Thou hast brought me to Sheol, the kingdom of death. I am become a man without God. Thy wrath lieth hard upon me. Thy wrath presseth, thou hast laid thy fury upon me. Thou hast let all thy waves strike me. I have called upon thee, my God, day and night; and thou hearest me not. I have borne thy terrors so that I am distracted—helpless. The outbursts of thy wrath, thy streams of wrath have cut me off'' (*Cross Reference Bible,* verses 6, 3, 5, 7, 9, 15, 16). No finite mind can ever comprehend the depth of anguish He endured during that seeming eternity in the nether abyss. It is probably best described in the words of the prophet, ''He hath poured out his soul unto death'' (Isa. 53:12). He suffered in our

stead, until, in the mind of God, the claims of etern
justice were fully met, as confirmed in Isaiah 53:11: "He
shall see of the travail of his soul, and shall be satisfied."

The Anguish of the Father

We marvel at Jesus' willingness to drink that awful cup
of woe—but we are in danger of forgetting that "God [the
Father] so loved the world that he *gave* his only begotten
Son." Jesus was not the only sufferer in the Godhead. It is
impossible to imagine what the Father suffered when He
had to forsake the Son of His love in order to provide a full
atonement for us. *This was the essence of Jesus'
punishment and of the Father's sorrow.* But the Father's
anguish had not in just the forsaking reached its dreadful
climax. Something of the cost to the Father is revealed in
Romans 8:32: "He that spared not his own Son, *but
delivered him up for us all,* how shall he not with him also
freely give us all things?" Eternal judgment against sin
could not be satisfied by merely turning His Son over to the
insufferable tortures of Satan. Justice required that the full
fury of the Father's own wrath against the cumulative sin
of the human race be poured out upon Him unto the
uttermost without stint or reservation—see again the
Psalm 88 passage already quoted.

*Imagine what it must have cost the Father to wreak the
full force of His wrath against the aggregate sin of all
mankind upon the innocent person of His beloved Son.*
From this there was no escape for the Father. This fact was
spelled out by Isaiah centuries before. "Yet it was the
Lord's good plan to bruise him and fill him with grief. But
when his soul has been made an offering for sin, then he
shall have a multitude of children, many heirs. He shall
live again and God's program shall prosper in his hands.
And when he [the Father] sees all that is accomplished by
the anguish of his soul, he [the Father] shall be satisfied;
and because of what he has experienced, my righteous

Servant shall make many to be counted righteous before
God, for he shall bear all their sins'' (Isa. 53:10-11 *LB*].
This was the immeasurable cost to the Father of obtaining a
truly generic seed, a family of His very very own, not
created only, as were the angels, but also generated
members of His very own household. And since Jesus
offered Himself ''through the eternal Spirit'' (Heb. 9:14),
all the members of the Godhead shared equally in the cost
of this amazing plan of redemption.

Christ's Conflict and Triumph in the Infernal Regions

When the claims of eternal justice were fully discharged
Christ was ''justified in the spirit'' (1 Tim. 3:16 *ASV*). He
then was ''made alive in the spirit'' (1 Peter 3:18 *ASV*).
His spirit was not annihilated. It only died spiritually like
any sinful human spirit. It was completely cut off and
separated from God. Thus, in order to be made alive unto
God and restored to fellowship with His Father, He had to
be reborn — for He had become the very essence of sin.
Since sin had totally alienated Him from the Father, the
only way He could be restored to fellowship with the Father
was through a new birth to new life. This is the meaning of
Revelation 1:5: ''Jesus Christ who is the first begotten
from among the dead'' (margin). As long as He was
identified with sin, He was in the clutches of Satan and the
hosts of hell, just like any lost sinner. But when He was
justified and made alive, adjudged and declared righteous in
the Supreme Court of the universe, the tables were turned.
The battle in that cavern of despair is described by Peter in
Acts 2:24: ''Whom God hath raised up, having loosed the
pains of death, because it was *not possible* that he should be
held by it'' (*NS*). This implies a tremendous effort on the
part of hell. When He, as an authentic man, had
completely disarmed and dethroned the arch foe of God and
man, He burst forth triumphantly from that age-old prison
of the dead. Paul says that He ''spoiled principalities and

powers" and "made a show of them openly, triumphing over them in it" (Col. 2:15). According to *Webster's New World Dictionary* this word "spoiled" means to "strip the hide from an animal," to "completely disarm a defeated foe," to "damage or injure in such a way as to make useless," to "destroy." This is what Jesus did to Satan after He was justified and made alive in the spirit. The monumental struggle that took place in that dark domain is implied in the words, "It was *not possible* that he should be held by it." Death did its utmost to shackle Him, to keep Him permanently in its grip. All of the resources of the underworld were mustered to prevent His resurrection, but in vain. It was impossible for death to "keep its prey." In the words of the psalm writer, "He hath broken the gates of brass, and cut the bars of iron in sunder" (Psalm 107:16). From that struggle He emerged triumphant with the keys of death and of hell. "I am he that liveth, and was dead; and, behold, I am alive for evermore, Amen; and have the keys of hell and of death" (Rev. 1:18).

Michelangelo has given us his conception of this event in one of his celebrated paintings. He shows the doorway of that ancient prison unhinged at Jesus' command, with a demon crushed beneath the fallen portal. Truly, "death could not hold Him." An eloquent writer has described the resurrection scene and Christ's ensuing exaltation thus: "Forcing a mighty earthquake, He mounted up again to solid earth, the light of day, and to the world of breathing men. Up and up again through the rent clouds and ranks of shouting angels and under the lifted heads of the everlasting doors, until He took His seat at the right hand of the Majesty in the heavens. In the realms of space, in the kingdoms of the universe, in the regions of light or darkness, in the epochs of eternity, there are none to rival our Lord Jesus and no power that does not owe Him tribute. In the nether abyss He has no unconquered challenger. In the heavenlies, it seems there are thrones higher and lower and names more or less eminent, but *He* stands clear above them all. The Christ who died on the cross, who rose from the grave in human form, is exalted as a human being to share the Father's glory and dominion, is filled with God's own fullness, and made without limitation or exception Head over *all* things." Yes, today an authentic human being sits on the throne of the universe, wielding all the authority of the Godhead.

Christ's Exaltation and the Church's Enthronement

When Christ took His seat in the heavens, He proved conclusively that Satan's devastation was complete, that he was utterly undone. Hell was thrown into total bankruptcy. Satan was not only stripped of his legal authority and dominion, but by an infinitely superior force he was stripped of his weapons also. But this is not all. When Jesus burst forth from that dark prison and "ascended up on high," all believers were raised and seated together with Him. "But God . . . brought us to life with Christ. . . . And in union with Christ Jesus he raised us up and enthroned us with him in the heavenly realms" (Eph. 2:4-6 *NEB*).

Identified With Christ in His Death and Resurrection

In the mind of God every believer shares complete identity with Christ from the cross to the throne. According to the Word, we are crucified with Him, buried with Him, raised with Him, exalted with Him, and enthroned with Him (Rom. 6 and Eph. 2). How is this understandable? Consider the following:

The total cumulative sin of the world could not be laid upon Him independent of the sinner himself. There is no such thing as abstract sin, sin apart from the sinner. Not only was the sinner's sin laid upon Him, but the person of the sinner as well. Therefore, when He went to the cross He carried the entire human race with Him. "We thus judge that if one died for all, then were all dead" (2 Cor. 5:14). "I have been crucified with Christ; and it is no longer I who live, but Christ lives in me" (Gal. 2:20 *NASV*). "It is a faithful saying: For if we be dead with him, we shall also live with him" (2 Tim. 2:11). All mankind was identified with Him in death, *but only those who believe are identified with Him in His resurrection and exaltation.*

Identified With Christ in His Exaltation and Enthronement

We are not surprised that *He* is exalted and enthroned in the heavens. What is difficult for us to comprehend is that *we* have been exalted with Him. Yet if "he that is joined unto the Lord is one spirit" (1 Cor. 6:17), it cannot be otherwise. We are not surprised that "all things have been put under *his* feet." What we have failed to comprehend is that as part of Him, His Body, all things are also legally beneath *our* feet. What we do not realize is that He is "the head over all things *to the church*" (Eph. 1:22). This means that *His Headship over all things is assumed and held for the benefit of the Church* and is directed toward His purpose for her. *We have underestimated the supreme importance of the Church in God's economy. She is the center and motive of all His activity from all eternity.* He does nothing solely for His own sake. She is included as a full partner in all His plans. The Church is His Body, the fullness of Him that fills all things everywhere. *He is not full or complete without His Church which is His Body.* This is true only because of God's voluntary self-limita-tion. In the absolute, God is wholly self-sufficient. He needs nothing and can be served by no one. Yet He has chosen voluntarily to limit Himself in order that the Church may become His judicial equal. It is true that the Body cannot function without the Head. It is just as true that the Head, by His own choice, cannot function without the Body. Both are equally important to the accomplishment of His plan.

Identified With Christ in His Conquest of Satan

The same truth is taught in the figure of the vine and the branches. While it is true that "the branch cannot bear fruit of itself, except it abide in the vine" (John 15:4), it is also true that the vine does not bear fruit without the branches on which the fruit appears. These are illustrations of God's voluntary limiting of Himself so that He not only needs the Church, but, due to the nature of the divine economy, He cannot accomplish His chosen goal without her. Because of God's free self-limitation, the Body is equally important as the Head for functioning, just as the branch is equally important as the vine for fruit bearing. *His voluntary self-limitation is for the purpose of making room for the members of His "Bridehood" to realize their full potential as generic sons of God.* His goal in His self-limitation is to inaugurate a process by which the members of the "Bridehood," as judicial equals, may eternally approximate the character of the Son, thus implementing His plan to "bring many sons to glory," to their highest potential as blood-brothers of the Eternal Son. He has taken us into His family as "His very own," that is, as generated members of His household as distinguished from other orders of beings who are only created, not generated. *Through the new birth we are the "next of kin."* We are organically a part of Christ. As a part of Him, when He conquered the forces of darkness and left them disarmed and paralyzed before He arose from the dead, we who believe were participants in that victory. When He snatched the keys of death and hell from Satan and burst forth from that nether abyss, we were sharers in that triumph. When He ascended up on high and took His seat in the heavenlies, we were exalted with Him. Because Satan and all the hosts of hell are beneath His feet, they are likewise beneath ours. *When He defeated Satan it was our victory. He did not conquer Satan for Himself. The entire substitutionary work of Christ was for His Bride-elect, the Church.* He became flesh and blood so that He could enter the conflict and overcome Satan as an unfallen human being for her benefit, not for His. *Therefore, we are Satan's masters. He can lord it over us no more.* His dominion over us ended at Calvary. *Instead of his having power over us, we have been given authority over him.* This is the meaning of our enthronement with Christ.

Satanic Guerrilla Warfare

One of our great difficulties, after we know who we are, is that under satanic pressure we so soon forget. For although Satan knows what Christ did to him at Calvary and through the Resurrection, and realizes that as a part of Christ the believer is his master, he still carries on a guerrilla warfare against the Church through the use of subterfuge, deception, and bluff. While guerrilla warfare is illegal, it is still warfare and must be faced and overcome. God could put Satan completely away, but He has chosen to use him to give the Church "on-the-job" training in overcoming. Otherwise, there would be no more warfare of any kind. We are in apprenticeship for our place with Christ on the throne following the Marriage Supper of the Lamb. The crown belongs to the conqueror — and without an adversary there could be no practice in overcoming. Thus, when God permits Satan to throw his black mantle over our spirits, we are in danger of forgetting who we are. We are like the man James tells us about, who looks at his face in a mirror, and looking at himself, goes away and immediately forgets what he looks like (Jas. 1:23-24). Because we forget so easily that we have passed from Satan's authority, we allow him to threaten and oppress us. We forget that we are actually a part of Christ and that Satan is subject to us. We unconsciously lapse into our old life of fear and defeat, seeing ourselves as we were and not as we are. We must constantly remind ourselves and affirm that we are in Christ — and because Satan cannot touch Christ, he cannot touch us.[2] "No one who has become a part of God's family makes a practice of sinning, for Christ, God's Son, holds him securely, and the devil cannot get his hands on him" (1 John 5:18 *LB*). Satan wants the believer to forget that he is risen and exalted with Christ, that he is now, in his real person, that is, his spirit, united with Christ on the throne with all enemies under his feet. If he is held in bondage to demons of fear, sickness, disease, or limitation of any kind, it is only by ignorance of what Christ has done for him, or by forgetting who he is.

Affirmation of Identity

We need constantly to remind ourselves of our identity by affirming: "Because I am a part of Christ, 'accepted in the Beloved,' I hold the same place in the Father's bosom as He does. Because I am a part of Christ, the Father loves me as much as He loves Christ (John 17:23,26). Because I am a part of Christ, I have His wisdom — because He is made wisdom to me (1 Cor. 1:30). Likewise I have His righteousness. My righteousness is as good as His in the eyes of the Father because it is *His* righteousness. Because I am organically a part of Him, because Head and Body are one unit, *all that Christ is and has is accredited to me.*"

It is the Father's purpose to make all of the sons as nearly equal with the Son as it is possible for the finite to be like the Infinite. This equality is to be first in character and then in privilege and power. It is to be not only legal and theoretical, but in essential reality. "For all who are led by the Spirit of God are sons of God. And so we should not be like fearful, cringing slaves, but we should behave like God's very own children. . . . And since we are his children, we will share his treasures — for all God gives to his Son Jesus is now ours too. But if we are to share his glory, we must also share his suffering'' (Rom. 8:14,17 *LB*).

The Unlimited Potential of the Church

All of this is assurance that it is God's intention that the Church militant should walk in the same life, power, and divine liberty as Jesus walked. ''As the Father hath sent me, even so send I you.'' This ''even so'' suggests that we are sent under the same circumstances, with the same authority, and with the same resources as the Father sent the Son. *God does not set any arbitrary limits to the Church's use of divine resources.* He has made available all that He is to a believing Church. ''Of his fulness have all we received'' (John 1:16). ''And to know the love of Christ, which passeth knowledge, that you might be filled with all the fulness of God'' (Eph. 3:19). *All limitation is on the part of the believer.* One saint realized the full potential of walking with God, clear up to translation. What one man did by faith, it is conceivable that others may do. God has given us the keys of the kingdom of heaven, but He does not compel us to use them. He waits. The rest is up to us, His Church. In His triumph over Satan He has given us the needed weapons. How well we use them is our responsibility and may well determine our rank in the Bridehood.

NOTES

1.   When Jesus cried ''It is finished,'' it was the end of the Mosaic covenant with its laws and ordinances which He completely fulfilled: ''Blotting out the handwriting of ordinances that was against us, which was contrary to us, and took it out of the way, nailing it to his cross. And, having spoiled principalities and powers [in his descent into hell], he made a show of them openly, triumphing over them in it'' (Col. 2:14-15). Sin is basically a spiritual thing, a thing of the spirit, and therefore must be dealt with in the spirit realm. If Jesus paid the full penalty of sin on the cross only, that is, by His physical death alone, then sin is wholly a physical act. If sin is wholly a physical act, then every man could pay for his own sin by his own death. Because sin is basically or primarily in the spirit realm and of the spirit, therefore Jesus' work was not finished when He yielded up His physical life on the cross. It was not completed until He descended into hell, paid once and for all the eternal consequences of the aggregate sin of the world, completely despoiled Satan and all the hosts of evil, arose triumphantly from the dead, and carried His blood into the heavenly Holy of Holies and sprinkled it upon the Mercy Seat there. Hallelujah!

2.   Job 1:9-12 reveals that except by God's permission Satan cannot touch us. He is entirely under God's control. Only when divine love permits may Satan have access to God's child. And the end result, for the tested believer, is always ''twice as much'' blessing as before (Job 42:10).

7

THE MYSTERY OF UNANSWERED PRAYER

And this is the confidence that we have in him, that, if we ask anything according to his will, he heareth us; and if we know that he hear us, whatsoever we ask, we know that we have the petitions that we desired of him (1 John 5:14-15).

This passage of Scripture declares that for God the Father to hear a prayer is the equivalent to His answering it. It is a divinely inspired syllogism. When we ask in the will of God it is logical that, since the request has come from God in the first place, He is even more interested in our receiving the answer than we can be. The syllogism might be stated thus: God has promised to hear and answer all prayers that are according to His will. My prayer is according to His will; therefore He has answered my prayer.

Why?

In the light of this and many other unequivocal promises to answer prayer, the question that arises is, "*Why* should there be any apparently unanswered prayers?" If Satan has been legally defeated, dethroned, disarmed, stripped of his weapons and "destroyed"; and if the Church has actually been exalted and enthroned with Christ, with all enemies beneath her feet; if she has been given "authority over all the power of the enemy" and has been deputized by God to enforce His will upon earth — *why* does she not more efficiently demonstrate the genuineness of her triumph in Christ?

It has been shown that the Church, by her prayers and faith, feeble as they are, is the controlling factor in human affairs; and that she holds the balance of power, not only in the social order, but also in the salvation of individual souls. Yet it is clear that she is not living up to her spiritual potential as set forth in the Word. What is the reason? Where does the fault lie?

God Thwarted by Selfish Motives

It must be settled once and for all that any reason for unanswered prayer is always on the human side. Most, if not all, Biblical writers assume that all prayers which are according to God's will are answered. Neither Jesus nor John acknowledges any such thing as unanswered prayer. "Ask, and it *shall* be given you; seek and ye *shall* find; knock, and it *shall* be opened unto you; for every one that asketh *receiveth;* and he that seeketh *findeth;* and to him that knocketh it *shall be opened*" (Matt. 7:7-8). "And whatsoever ye shall ask in my name, *that* will I do.... If ye shall ask anything in my name, I will do *it*" (John 14:13-14). Also 1 John 5:14-15 at the head of the chapter.

In spite of these unequivocal promises, we do have some references in the Word to unanswered prayer. (I call these unequivocal because there are no unreasonable conditions attached.) While James acknowledges the fact of unanswered prayer, he clearly indicates that the reason is on the human side. "Ye ask, and receive not, because ye ask amiss, that ye may consume it upon your lusts" (Jas. 4:3).

Refusal of Paul's Request

Paul reports a case of unanswered prayer in his own life, but he also explains that the reason was on the human side.

"And lest I should be exalted above measure through the abundance of the revelations, there was given me a thorn in the flesh, the messenger of Satan to buffet me, lest I should be exalted above measure" (2 Cor. 12:7). Paul further informs us that he besought the Lord three times to take it away but without success. The Lord refused, and for a reason.

Although this is the only case of its kind in the New Testament, it may illustrate a principle which operates almost universally. Ego exaltation is probably the most dangerous and deadly of sins. It caused the downfall of Lucifer, with all of its attending tragedies. It made the original earth a chaos, drowned in stygian darkness. It upset the balance of an entire planet. For any created being to make itself or any other thing but God the center of his world is catastrophic and self-destructive. Satan, who was once Lucifer, is an illustration. Before his fall, he was the highest of all pre-Adamic created beings. According to Isaiah 14 and Ezekiel 28 he was the guardian of the throne of God, "the anointed cherub that covereth," "full of wisdom and perfect in beauty." Being next to God Himself, says Ezekiel, Lucifer's heart was lifted up (filled with pride) because of his beauty and his wisdom was corrupted because of his brightness (splendor or brilliance). Verse 18 in *The Living Bible* reads: "You defiled your holiness with lust for gain; therefore I brought forth fire from your own actions and let it burn you to ashes." His covetousness and greed, his ambition for power, were so fired by the supreme gifts God had showered upon him that his personality disintegrated. The inner fires kindled by his conceit and self-worship "burned him to ashes." *This is the general pattern of self-destruction.* Paul recognized this danger when he cautioned Timothy that a bishop must not be a novice or a new convert "in case he becomes conceited and incurs the doom passed on the devil" (1 Tim. 3:6

Moffatt). Satan seeks to produce the "Lucifer syndrome" in every believer because he knows it will bring upon him what Paul calls "the condemnation of the devil" (1 Tim. 3:6). Conceit is always from the devil and is one of his most devastating tools. Paul recognized this by pinpointing the danger of his becoming conceited because of the "abundance of the revelations" given to him (2 Cor. 12:7). Certainly no one in this dispensation was ever taken into the councils of the Trinity as Paul was. To counteract the danger of being "exalted above measure" and hence falling into the "condemnation of the devil," Paul was given the "thorn" and his request for its removal was refused as a safety measure.

God Thwarted by Spiritual Pride

While Paul's situation was totally unique, the principle governing it may be more general. Very few can take honors, either from the world or from God, without becoming conceited. What servant of the Lord does not know the subtle temptation to spiritual pride that follows even mediocre success? How often one relates an answer to prayer in such a way as to reflect credit upon oneself—and then ends up blandly saying "To God be the glory." The ego is so swollen by the fall that it is an easy prey to Satan and his demons. As C. S. Lovett has said, they lurk constantly "just outside your skin" and they take advantage of the smallest provocation to inflate the fallen psyche. Who knows how much God would do for His servants if He dared. If one does not boast openly following an anointed fluency of speech, a specific answer to prayer, a miracle of faith or some other manifestation of spiritual gifts, or even graces, he is tempted to gloat secretly because of the recognition. Except for special grace on such occasions, one falls easily into Satan's trap. Because most men are so vulnerable to any small stimulus to pride, God, although He loves to do so, dares not honor many before the world by special displays of His miracle-working power in answer to prayer.

This does not mean that God has repudiated His promise when such requests seem to be refused, but that human weakness and infirmity frustrates Him and prevents the answer, that is ready and waiting, from arriving. If God felt compelled to withhold from Paul the answer to his prayer to prevent his being "exalted above measure," may this explain why God cannot answer more prayers for His children? The sands of time are strewn with the wrecks of the broken lives of many who were once mightily used of God, but who suffered shipwreck upon the rocks of spiritual pride. This explains why Watchman Nee says that God's great work is to reduce *us,* that is, our ego. For until God has wrought a work of true humility and brokenness in His servants, He can not answer some of their prayers without undue risk of producing the pride that goes before a fall. If God could trust the petitioner to keep lowly, who knows how many more answers to prayer He would readily give.

This principle may also explain why answers to prayer for healing sometimes are not received. If the answer to prayer for healing in Paul's case was hazardous to him, how much more so may it be in many others. Although no one since Paul has ever had as much reason to be exalted because of the abundance of revelations, very few have his ability to keep humble. Is it possible that one reason why some are not healed is that God sees they too might be lifted up with spiritual pride and "fall into the condemnation of the devil"? If God felt it advisable to withhold the answer to Paul's prayer for healing to keep him humble, may this not explain the failure of some other prayers for healing?

God Thwarted By Prayerlessness

In previous chapters it is averred that the authority over

Satan and his hierarchy which Christ delegated to His Church operates wholly within the framework and system of believing prayer which God has ordained. By God's own choice, all of this vast delegated authority is wholly inoperative apart from the prayers of a believing Church. If the Church does not pray God will not act, because that would nullify His plan to prepare her for rulership through "on-the-job" training in enforcing Christ's victory at Calvary. If it were not for His determination to bring her up to full stature as His co-regent, God would not have established the system of prayer at all. There is no intrinsic power in prayer as such. On the contrary, prayer is an acknowledgement of need, of helplessness. If He chose, He could act arbitrarily without regard to prayer or lack of it. All power originates in God and belongs to Him alone. *He ordained prayer not primarily as a means of getting things done for Himself, but as part of the apprenticeship program for training the Church for her royal duties which will follow the Marriage Supper of the Lamb. Unless she understands this and enters into sincere cooperation with God's plan of prayer, the power needed to overcome and bind Satan on earth will not be released.* God has the power to overcome Satan without the cooperation of His Church through prayer and faith, but if He did it without her it would deprive her of enforcement practice and rob her of the strength she would gain in overcoming. This is God's primary reason for inaugurating the system of prayer and unequivocally binding Himself to answer. *Therefore, there is no authority apart from persistent believing prayer.*

Great Organizers — Poor Pray-ers

To the extent that the Church fails to realize this and give herself to prayer and intercession, to that extent she ties God's hands and forfeits her right to answered prayer. This brings us to the greatest reason for the paucity of answers to prayer: *prayerlessness* itself. "Ye have not because ye ask not.'' Earlier it was pointed out that the social order has been preserved from total decay even though so few pray so little. The Church's prayerlessness needs no proof. Each man stands convicted at the bar of his own conscience. The days of the David Brainerds, the Praying Hydes, the Father Nashes, and the E. M. Boundses sometimes appear to be past. The Western church has lost the prayer stamina of the mission churches in Asia, Africa, South America, Indonesia, and those of the underground church behind the Iron Curtain. Yes, we are great organizers but poor pray-ers. *Neglect of prayer is one reason for so few answers.*

Ecclesiastical Treadmills

The average local church provides an intelligent educational program through the Sunday School and such auxiliaries as the Vacation Bible School. It may provide well-directed youth programs, including social activities and recreational Bible camps. It may sponsor Teacher Training and Personal Evangelism classes. Many churches launch great evangelistic campaigns, featuring big-name evangelistic parties with a high potential of religious entertainment. Many have an efficient, well-structured, and highly successful stewardship and financial program. All of these may be working smoothly, and in high gear.

This is not to discount any of these programs per se. They may be good. *But if they are substitutes for an effective prayer program, they may be useless so far as damaging Satan's kingdom is concerned.* A church without an intelligent, well-organized, and systematic prayer program is simply operating a religious treadmill. One fears that this is an appropriate description of most church programs today. If we could see as God sees, we would behold a great forest of giant ecclesiastical treadmills operating in depth all over the United States and in many other parts of the world. Such an operation may be very exhilarating. It may employ enormous manpower, absorb almost limitless time, and demand a huge financial budget. It may give an illusion of accomplishment and success. It may flatter the ego. *But any church program, no matter how impressive, if it is not supported by an adequate prayer program, is little more than an ecclesiastical treadmill.* It is doing little or no damage to Satan's kingdom.

Prayer Is Where the Action Is

If our theology of prayer is scriptural, then PRAYER IS WHERE THE ACTION IS. John Wesley was correct when he said, "God does nothing but in answer to prayer." Also S. D. Gordon when he said, "Prayer is striking the winning blow. . . . Service is gathering up the results." And E. M. Bounds was right when he said, "God shapes the world by prayer. The prayers of God's saints are the capital stock of heaven by which God carries on His great work upon earth." There was a time when I doubted these claims. Only when I came to understand more fully the deeper aspects of the theology of prayer was I convinced of their truth. Since they are true, then indeed prayer *is* where the action is.

Israel and Amalek

This fact is illustrated in the conflict between Israel and Amalek. God had brought Israel out of Egypt and was leading her toward the promised land for the purpose of developing her into the Messianic nation. Satan, the great enemy of God and His Messianic program, sought at this point to hinder the further progress of Israel toward the land. He stirred up the heathen nation of Amalek, a descendant of Ishmael, and sought to use the Amalekites as his instruments of opposition. As the battle was being joined, Moses said to Joshua, "Choose us out men, and go out, fight with Amalek: tomorrow I will stand on the top of the hill with the rod of God in mine hand." So Joshua did as Moses had said and fought with Amalek. "And Moses,

Aaron, and Hur went up to the top of the hill. And it came to pass, when Moses held up his hand, that Israel prevailed; and when he let down his hand, Amalek prevailed'' (Ex. 17:9-11). You know the rest of the story. When Moses grew weary and had to rest his arms, Aaron and Hur stood on either side and supported him until Amalek was completely defeated and God's plan for the Messianic nation proceeded.

A Mountain-top Victory

To the superficial observer the action was on the battlefield where the troops were in combat. But the spiritually discerning mind knows that the real battle was fought, and the victory won, up on the mount where Moses, Aaron, and Hur were unitedly holding aloft the rod of God, symbol of His power. The Amalekites were merely the tools of Satan. They were controlled and inspired by satanic forces. When the three intercessors on the mount unitedly engaged in believing prayer, the demonic forces motivating the Amalekites were bound and they were paralyzed. Then Israel prevailed. But when weariness compelled Moses to rest, the evil spirits were released and again energized Israel's foes. Therefore, Aaron and Hur united with Moses and strengthened him, assisting to hold up his hands in intercession until the going down of the sun. Thus, it is said, Joshua vanquished Amalek. But the *real* action was on the top of the hill. There the evil spirits were bound so that Joshua and Israel could prevail. ''The winning blow'' was struck on the height of intercession. Joshua and Israel merely ''gathered up the results.'' Therefore, prayer *is* where the action is.

Since this is true, then prayer becomes the highest privilege of the redeemed because it places the intercessor as truly at the front line of spiritual conflict and conquest as the pastor, evangelist, missionary, or any other soldier of the cross. Moreover, the weapons available to him are as effective as those available to the most potent spiritual leader. As S. D. Gordon has said, "Prayer puts one in touch with a planet. I can as really be touching hearts for God in far away India or China through prayer as though I were there." He says further, "A man may go aside today, and shut his door, and as really spend a half hour in India for God . . . as though he were there in person" (*Quiet Talks On Prayer*). In other words, prayer has no space or geographical limitations. This is why Alexander Maclaren has said, in speaking of the mission field, that much prayer for the cause by those at the home base means power released on the field, and that weakness at home means weakness on the field.

Prayer — Not Personality

Does anyone imagine that souls are delivered from Satan's bondage by means of human talent, the hypnotic power of human personality, the charm of human magnetism, eloquence, articulateness, or the magic of Madison Avenue techniques? All of these gifts God may use, but alone they are utterly powerless to deliver even one soul from the captivity of sin. "The flesh profiteth nothing" (John 6:63).

Prayer — Not Eloquence

From heaven's standpoint, all spiritual victories are won, not primarily in the pulpit, not primarily in the klieg light of publicity, nor yet through the ostentatious blaring of trumpets, but in the secret place of prayer. The only power that overcomes Satan and releases souls from his stranglehold is *the power of the Holy Spirit,* and the only power that releases the energy of the Holy Spirit is *the power of believing prayer.* Thank God for the gifts, talents, and preaching ability of men like Billy Graham. This is no effort to depreciate these assets. But the power that has transformed multiplied thousands through Billy Graham's ministry is not the power of superior gifts, unusual talents, brilliant rhetoric, or psychological persuasiveness, but the power released by the prayer and faith of the millions of his prayer helpers. From heaven's standpoint, the combined prayer and intercession which surrounds and supports Billy Graham is the real explanation of what is taking place. Because of the immense program of prayer warfare on his behalf, Satan's legions opposing his efforts are overcome and bound in the same way they were when Moses, Aaron, and Hur interceded for Joshua and Israel against Amalek.

Prayer — Not Art

Since this is true, the spiritual effectiveness of the message of those in the pulpit and those on the radio and television is not the result, primarily, of their superior platform or program techniques, or even the profound content of their message. These should not be discounted. The lack of them may greatly hinder. *But the power that binds Satan and transforms men is released only by earnest, believing prayer.* The same may be said about the message of a book. The art and skill of the author is important. But the message is sealed unless the Holy Spirit opens and quickens it to the minds of the readers. Here again, prayer is the secret of effectiveness because PRAYER IS WHERE THE ACTION IS.

Prayer and Reward

Many people grieve because they have been denied service on the mission field or in some other chosen endeavor. *Through faithful intercession they may accomplish as much and reap as full a reward as though they had been on the field in person.* Those who lament that they have been cheated in life because they have no shining gifts or spectacular talents, or those who have been retired by age or illness, may, through faithful intercession, share in the heavenly reward equally with the most highly endowed, all because PRAYER IS WHERE THE ACTION IS. "He that receiveth a prophet in the name of a prophet shall receive a prophet's reward; and he that receiveth a righteous man in the name of a righteous man shall receive a righteous man's reward'' (Matt. 10:41). If simple hospitality brings equal compensation, then a prayer support ministry will surely not go unrewarded.

No Room for Self-pity

This leaves no room for self-pity or envy of those more gifted, provided one is willing to fill his place as a prayer warrior. *In heaven's "book" the nameless saint in the most remote and secluded spot, completely lost to view, and overshadowed in the battle, is just as important, and if he is faithful, will receive just as great a reward, as the most heralded and gifted leader. Hallelujah!* All of the faithful prayer warriors are just as truly at the front and are making just as great a contribution in the fray as the apparent leader. And they will share equally in the reward. Verily, "The fate of the world is in the hands of nameless saints."

Daniel's Intercession

Another illustration of this truth is recorded in Daniel, chapter ten. Again the mission of the Messianic nation was in view. The vision concerning the future of the nation came to Daniel at the close of a three week period of fasting. During all of that time Daniel was in mourning for his people; that is, he was engaged in prayer and intercession concerning the future of Israel. When at last the angel appeared with the message from heaven, he revealed to Daniel the astounding reason for the long delay. Daniel's prayer was heard in heaven the very day that he began his intercession and immediately this heavenly messenger was dispatched with the answer. But he was intercepted. *The Living Bible* paraphrases it this way: "That very day I was sent here to meet you. But for twenty-one days the mighty Evil Spirit who overrules the kingdom of Persia blocked my way. Then Michael, one of the top officers of the heavenly army, came to help me, so that I was able to break through these spirit rulers of Persia'' (Dan. 10:12-13).

Battle in the Spirit World

Here is a historical account of a literal conflict in the unseen realms. It is doubtless the pattern of many similar conflicts that rage constantly in the spirit world. It is the story of an action on two levels. Down by the river is a man in fasting and prayer. He labors, he pleads, he insists, he persists, he importunes, wrestles, and agonizes. He is in mourning day after day. He has read Jeremiah's prophecy of the seventy years of captivity and knows that the time has almost expired. The time for the fulfillment is almost here. Although God is sovereign and could, if He chose, fulfill His prophecies unaided, Daniel evidently realized that intercession had a part to play in bringing the prophecy to pass. God had made the prophecy. *When it was time for its fulfillment He did not fulfill it arbitrarily outside of His program of prayer. He sought for a man upon whose heart He could lay a burden of intercession.* Intercession is the most unselfish thing anyone can do.

As always, God made the decision in heaven. A man was called upon to enforce that decision on earth through intercession and faith. This part of the conflict—the prayer sessions by the river—is on a level which we can observe. But another part of the battle was invisible from earth. While Daniel was on his face interceding, a concomitant conflict, a related pitched battle, was raging in the heavens. Two angels, and possibly the spirit forces under their command, were engaged in a fierce combat which continued for three weeks. Since God does nothing but in answer to prayer, if Daniel had grown weary and become discouraged, God would have been compelled to find someone else to intercede or permit His messenger to suffer defeat. Although the answer to his prayer was granted and already on the way, if Daniel had given up it presumably would never have arrived. Therefore the real battle was fought and the victory won in the place of prayer down on the river bank. The decisive action was there.

The "Why" of Importunity

This Biblical account suggests a principle which may explain many apparently unanswered prayers. Since our promise in 1 John, chapter 5, is true, every prayer offered in faith according to God's will is always answered in heaven. This passage says so. But Satan never allows an answer to reach earth if he can prevent it. *Persistence and importunity in prayer are not needed to persuade a willing God but to enable Him to overcome opposition of hindering evil spirits.* If God's purpose in His prayer program is to give us "on-the-job" training in overcoming Satan, He cannot arbitrarily remove the demonic hindrances. If He went over the Church's head, took the matter out of her hands, and won the victory for her, it would prevent her growth unto full stature and qualifying for the throne as an overcomer. *This is the reason for the Biblical teaching on the importance of importunity.* The answer to many prayers that have already been granted in heaven may never be received because the petitioner becomes weary, discouraged, or intimidated, and gives up the fight. Jesus tells us that the man who needed three loaves from his neighbor received them because of his importunity. And then He adds: "Ask, and keep on asking, and it shall be given you; seek, and keep on seeking, and you shall find; knock, and keep on knocking, and the door shall be opened to you" (Luke 11:9 *Amplified*). The word from God to Habakkuk the prophet is pertinent here: "The vision has its own appointed hour, it ripens, it will flower; if it be long then wait, for it is sure, and it will not be late" (Hab. 2:3 *Moffatt*). *One reason many prayers are apparently unanswered is the failure of the petitioner to continue with importunity until the answer is received.*

On this point S. D. Gordon, in his *Quiet Talks On*

Prayer, says, "It is a fiercely contested conflict. Satan is a trained strategist, and an obstinate fighter. He refuses to acknowledge defeat until he must. It is the fight for his life. . . . The enemy yields only what he must. He yields only what is taken. Therefore, the ground must be taken step by step. . . . He continually renews his attacks, therefore the ground taken must be held against him in the VICTOR'S Name." "Wherefore, take unto you the whole armor of God, that ye may be able to withstand in the evil day, and having done all, to stand. Stand, therefore, having your loins girded about with truth, and having on the breastplate of righteousness [integrity]" (Eph. 6:13-14 *NS*). *It is a conflict of wills.* If Satan's will, persistence, and determination outlasts that of the petitioner, the petitioner is defeated. But the petitioner has the advantage because of Christ's victory and never needs to suffer defeat. *Importunity combined with perfect faith is unconquerable.*

The Cause of Prayerlessness

Thus far we have emphasized prayerlessness and lack of importunity as reasons for ineffective prayer. In the light of God's many unequivocal promises to answer prayer, the question arises: *Why* is the prayer activity of the Church so sadly neglected? What is the reason for the Church's prayerlessness? Many reasons could be suggested but perhaps the most basic one is LACK OF FAITH IN THE INTEGRITY OF THE WORD OF GOD. If the Church were fully convinced of the fulfillment of the promises — such as: "Ask, and it *shall* be given you; seek, and ye *shall* find; knock, and it *shall* be opened unto you" (Matt. 7:7) — prayer would be the main business of her life. *Unbelief in the integrity of the Word is the first great cause for prayerlessness.* This unbelief is so deep-seated as to be unconscious, but it is betrayed by the feeble prayer life of the Church.

A Proper Evaluation of the Word

We need a proper evaluation of the Word. According to Erich Sauer in *The King of the Earth,* man's spiritual nature expresses itself chiefly in his power of speech. "Speech is the direct self-revelation of the inward man or of the personality. Thought is, as it were, the inward speech of the spirit and the spoken or written word forms a body for the thought. Speech is the instrument for the manifestation of the spirit." Your thought is you. "For as [a man] *thinketh in his heart, so is he*" (Prov. 23:7). *If thought is an integral part of the person, as this passage teaches, then speech also must be, because it is the body of thought. Therefore, God's Word must be truly a part of Himself and God Himself actually lives in His Word.*

We must recognize, of course, that in the most basic sense, Jesus Christ is the Word. He is the Word who was with the Father in the beginning (John 1:1). He is spoken of as the *Logos* or Word because it is He who perfectly reveals the Father. "No man hath seen God at any time; the only begotten Son, which is in the bosom of the Father, he hath declared him" (John 1:18).

We today, however, do not have the eternal Word living among us in the flesh. But we do have His counterpart, the Comforter whom He sent, the Holy Spirit (John 16:7). The Holy Spirit has inspired the written revelation of God's nature and acts which we have today and know as the Bible. "All Scripture is God-breathed and is useful for teaching, rebuking, correcting and training in righteousness, so that the man of God may be thoroughly equipped for every good work" (2 Tim. 3:16-17 *New International Version*). Though He used prepared human instruments to do the actual writing, what is written is truly the Word of God. This written Word of God forms a body for the thought of God. The written Word is not just "words," but is animated by His divine breath. It is therefore *alive*

(Heb. 4:12), a manifestation of God, a "body" for the Holy Spirit. In this sense it is truly a part of God Himself, and God actually lives in His Word.

The written Word is taking Jesus' place today. It is impregnated with His personality. It has all of the elements in it that were in Jesus. *Since the words of Jesus are actually a part of Him, all of the power and authority that He possesses is latent in His written Word.* The written Word carries the same authority as Jesus' spoken word. *Therefore, this living Word on the lips of absolute faith unmixed with doubt, spoken by a holy man sheer out of touch with Satan, totally out of sympathy with him—that spoken Word carries the same authority as when spoken by Jesus Himself.* If it were not for the Church's deep-seated unbelief, she would be demonstrating this constantly. And, thank God, it is being demonstrated today by those who truly believe.[1]

God is both author and energizer of this Word. You cannot separate God from His Word. This is why Jesus could say, "The scripture cannot be broken" (John 10:35). Because it is God-breathed, it cannot fail without dethroning God. If God would not keep His word that goes out of His mouth, He would not be God.

Cure for Prayerlessness

Since the above is so, the caution against Bibliolatry by some so-called Bible scholars is superfluous. Some of them charge that reverence for the Bible as the inerrant Word of God is a form of idolatry. In the light of the foregoing and of what God Himself says of His Word, can this be possible? "God is not a man, that he should lie; neither the son of man, that he should repent. Hath he said, and shall he not do it? Or hath he spoken, and shall he not make it good?" (Num. 23:19). "I watch over my word to perform it" (Jer. 1:12 *ASV*). The writer of the letter to the Hebrews declares that it is impossible for God to lie

(Heb. 6:18). In John 10:35 Jesus Himself states unequivocally that "the scripture *cannot* be broken." He further placed His seal upon the accuracy of the Scriptures when He said to the Jews, "They testify of me" (John 5:39). He Himself vouched for their integrity when He said, "Thy word is truth" (John 17:17). God's own reverence for His Word is proclaimed in this most astonishing declaration: "Thou hast magnified thy word above all thy name" (Psa. 138:2). We may not fully understand the meaning of this passage, but it testifies to God's supreme commitment to His Word. His honor is inseparably united with it. *Were the Church to believe fully in the integrity of God's Word, it would cure her prayerlessness.*

Success of Perfect Faith

Therefore, all apparently unanswered prayer that is according to God's will may be explained by Satan's deception, bluff, and opposition plus the believer's blindness, ignorance, timidity, personal character defects, and failure to persist in undaunted, unwavering faith. Since God is God, the responsibility for unanswered prayer cannot be laid at heaven's door. "Let God be true, but every man a liar" (Rom. 3:4). "God that cannot lie" (Titus 1:2). "The scripture cannot be broken" (John 10:35). Let us no longer cast any reflection upon the integrity of the Word. *Faith will never be perfected until we accept our responsibility for failure. The mystery of unanswered prayer is failure on the human side alone.* Alexander Maclaren says that if we understood ourselves better, and could see as God sees, we would trace all of our unanswered prayers to defects in our own Christian character. Thus, as the believer continues to seek God with a fully submitted will and to walk in all of the light as it comes, he may have boundless assurance that he shall, without fail, *when faith is perfected*, receive the answer for which he has prayed. As long as answers are delayed he can know that faith is deficient because "According to your faith be it unto you (Matt. 9:29). "If ye have faith, and doubt not, . . . ye shall say unto this mountain, Be thou removed, and be thou cast into the sea, [and] it shall be done" (Matt. 21:21). *"What things soever ye desire, when ye pray, believe that ye receive them and ye shall have them"* (Mark 11:24). "All things are possible to him that believeth" (Mark 9:23). *Jesus evidently does not acknowledge any such thing as unanswered prayer.* Many things may hinder perfect faith, but when faith is perfected the answer is received. This is an infallible divine law. *The mystery of unanswered prayer is explained by human failure alone, and ultimately by the failure of an imperfect faith.*

NOTES

1. Controversy surrounds the reports of the revival that began in 1965 on the Indonesian island of Timor. Some competent observers of the scene feel that events have been greatly exaggerated. Others insist that practically every miracle that characterized the first century Church is being repeated in our generation among those who are simple enough to "believe and doubt not." According to eyewitnesses, some who are unable to read or write are instruments in reproducing the most amazing of the Biblically recorded miracles. This confirms the words of Jesus, "I thank thee, O Father, Lord of heaven and earth, that thou hast hid these things from the wise and prudent, and hast revealed them unto babes" (Luke 10:21). What blessing may we be losing because of our religious sophistication which paralyzes genuine faith!

8

THE PROBLEM OF FAITH

Jesus said unto him, If thou canst believe, all things are possible to him that believeth (Mark 9:23).

The problem of a living faith, of faith without doubt, is a very real one. Many who have deep devotional habits and who live disciplined lives of prayer and intercession are never quite sure that they have prevailed because their faith seems tentative, dim, uncertain, and often mixed with doubt. Large segments of the Body of Christ are baffled by this plague. Much of the effectiveness of many well-organized prayer programs is crippled by failure to reach a triumphant faith. Since few know how to obtain and exercise this achieving faith, many prayer efforts bog down in frustration and defeat. *How* can this difficulty be overcome?

Praise Is the Answer

We have had much teaching on prayer, but until recently have had little on praise. Yet there is much more emphasis in the Bible on praise than on prayer. In the Bible, the entire universe, animate and inanimate, is envisioned as one grand chorus of praise to the Creator. Notice especially Psalms 148—150. Psalm 145:10 declares that "*All* thy works shall praise thee." *Praise is the highest occupation of angels. Heaven is one grand paean of praise*. Cherubim and seraphim unceasingly adore Him. "And the four living creatures had each of them six wings about him, and they were full of eyes within; and they rest not day and night, saying, Holy, Holy, Holy, Lord God Almighty, who was, and is, and is to come" (Rev. 4:8 NS). "And I beheld, and I heard the voice of many angels round about the throne and the living creatures and the elders, and the number of them was ten thousand times ten thousand, and thousands of thousands, saying with a loud voice, *Worthy is the Lamb!*" (Rev. 5:11-12 NS). "And I heard, as it were, the voice of a great multitude, and like the voice of many waters, and like the voice of mighty peals of thunder, saying, *Hallelujah! For the Lord God Omnipotent reigneth*" (Rev. 19:6 NS). Surely that which occupies the total time and energies of heaven must be a fitting pattern for earth.

Practical Aspects of Praise

For some reason the Church at large has underestimated the importance of praise. Many have had the idea that praise is a beautiful aesthetic exercise but has little practical value. But if praise is the highest occupation of angels there must be some valid reason for it. If heaven considers it important to maintain a chorus of praise unceasingly day and night around the throne (Rev. 4:8), it must be supremely efficacious. Would God tolerate an activity and exercise in heaven that is futile and irrational? We shall look, therefore, at some of the practical aspects of praise.

Praise and Character Development

If the highest function of angelic hosts is praise, it follows logically that the highest function of the human spirit must also be praise. Ever-increasing approximation to the infinitely lovely character of God is the most sublime goal of all creation. This is the *summum bonum*, the greatest good, the highest joy, the most exquisite delight, the supreme rapture, and the most ravishing transport of the human spirit. Just as antagonism, hostility, and cursing against God exercises and strengthens all that is most abominable, diabolical, and base in the human spirit, so worship and praise of the infinitely lovely God exercises, reinforces, and strengthens all that is most sublime, transcendent, and divine in the inner being. Thus as one worships and praises, he is continually transformed step by step, from glory to glory, into the image of the infinitely happy God. And the process can be expected to continue eternally. Therefore, praise is the most useful occupation and activity in enabling God to realize the supreme goal of the universe, that of "bringing many sons unto glory."

Praise and Mental Health

In recent years the subject of mental health among believers has received much attention. In the world at large, it is alleged, over half of the available hospital beds are occupied by victims of mental and nervous disorders. To deal with this problem great mental-health institutions have been constructed and the profession of psychiatry has been developed. It is my belief that a massive program of personal and corporate praise could put a large number of psychiatrists out of business and empty many mental institutions. The quintessence of all of our mental and nervous disorders is over-occupation with the personal ego; namely, self-centeredness. When the personality becomes centripetal, that is, ego-centered, it disintegrates. Out of extreme self-centeredness arises defensiveness, hostility, and aggressive antisocial behavior. According to the psychiatrists, these are the symptoms of mental sickness which require one to be hospitalized. To make one's self his center is self-destructive. Jesus affirmed this principle when He said, "Whosoever would save his life shall lose it, but whosoever will lose his life for my sake, the same shall save it" (Luke 9:24 *NS*).

Praise Decentralizes the Self

Here is one of the greatest values of praise: it decentralizes self. The worship and praise of God demands a shift of center from self to God. One cannot praise without relinquishing occupation with self. When praise becomes a way of life, the infinitely lovely God becomes the center of worship rather than the bankrupt self. Thus the personality becomes properly integrated and destructive stresses and strains disappear. This results in mental wholeness. Praise produces forgetfulness of self — and forgetfulness of self is health.

Praise Less Costly

One may pay a psychiatrist seventy-five dollars an hour to listen and look wise, and come away poorer and no better. But when a born-again believer suffering with depression and other emotional stresses turns to the infinitely lovely and all-wise God and applies himself diligently to worship and praise, a healing process begins. Praise, therefore, is something more than a vacuous religious form. It is the most practical and rewarding of occupations.

Praise and Domestic Peace

This principle has a most happy application in the home, where stresses and strains most often threaten disruption. There is nothing like praise to dispel self-pity, defensiveness, and hostility. Praise and such domestic vices are totally incompatible. One cannot praise and sulk. Praise and irritation cannot coexist. A massive program of individual praise will make a marriage counselor superfluous and could greatly reduce the load of divorce courts.

A Biblical Illustration

There are other reasons why praise is of such supreme importance and why so much larger a portion of the Word is given to praise than to prayer. *For some reason, Satan fears praise even more than prayer.* This is gloriously illustrated in 2 Chronicles chapter 20. A confederacy of Moab, Ammon, and the inhabitants of Mt. Seir declared war on Jehoshaphat, king of Judah. He immediately called the nation to repentance, fasting, and prayer. People from all across the nation gathered in Jerusalem for a great prayer meeting. As a result, through Jahaziel the prophet, God assured Jehoshaphat and the nation that they would achieve victory without a battle. The engagement is described in verses 20-22: "And they rose early in the morning, and went forth into the wilderness of Tekoa; and as they went forth, Jehoshaphat stood and said, Hear me, O Judah, and ye inhabitants of Jerusalem. Believe in the Lord your God, so shall ye be established; believe his prophets, so shall ye prosper. And when he had consulted with the people, he appointed *singers* unto the Lord, and that should *praise* the beauty of holiness, as they went out before the army, and to say, *Praise the Lord;* for his mercy endureth forever. And when they began to sing and to praise, the Lord set ambushments against the children of Ammon, Moab, and Mount Seir, which were come against Judah; and they were smitten.''

An Army Commits Suicide

Why was praise so effective in this situation? *It is because this was a spiritual conflict, a conflict between unseen spirits.* Since Judah was the Messianic nation, Satan had inspired and motivated this confederacy of nations to destroy Judah — in an effort to prevent the coming of the Messiah. But Jehoshaphat's prayer-and-praise program was more devastating to the enemy than an armed assault. Supported by the nationwide program of fasting and prayer, the praise of the choir and the ambush of the Lord so discomfited and confused the evil spirits animating their enemies that they became disoriented, confounded, and deranged, falling into insane, hysterical, and uncontrollable panic. In this state they turned upon one another and completely annihilated themselves. The entire hostile army "committed suicide."

Why Is Praise So Effective Against Satan?

Mrs. Frances Metcalf, in her little book *Making His Praise Glorious,* has called attention to the passages of Scripture which inform us that God's dwelling place is "between the cherubim": Psalm 80:1, 99:1, and Isaiah 37:16. While these passages refer to the cherubim covering the Ark of the Covenant, those cherubim are only an earthly reflection of the heavenly reality. They take their significance from the cherubim which surround the throne of the majesty on high, who rest not day and night, saying "Holy, holy, holy, Lord God Almighty." God dwells in an aura, an atmosphere, an enswathement of praise. Praise and His presence have a mutual affinity. Although God is omnipresent, He is not everywhere present in benign influence. Where there is joyful praise, there He is dynamically and benevolently active. In Psalm 22:3 we are told that God "inhabits the praises" of His people. This means that wherever there is adoration, reverence, and acceptable worship and praise, there He identifies and openly manifests His presence. *And His presence always expels Satan.* Satan cannot operate in the divine ambience. For years many have known that *praise is power* without fully understanding why. May this not be the explanation? Is it not a convincing rationale for praise? In short, *Satan is allergic to praise, so where there is massive, triumphant praise, Satan is paralyzed, bound, and banished.* [1]

The secret of overcoming faith, therefore, is *praise.* It was James who said, "Resist the devil, and he will flee from you" (Jas. 4:7). Since praise produces the atmosphere in which the Divine Presence resides, it is the most effective shield against Satan and satanic attack. Because praise is anathema to Satan, it is the most powerful defense, the most devastating weapon in conflict with him. Thus praise assures victory in prayer because it overcomes Satan, who is the great antagonist in prayer warfare.

The Importance of Continuous Massive Praise

The praise which overcomes is not merely occasional or spasmodic praise, praise that fluctuates with moods and circumstances. *It is continuous praise, praise that is a vocation, a way of life.* "I will bless [praise] the Lord at *all times;* his praise shall *continually* be in my mouth" (Psa. 34:1). "Blessed are they that dwell in thy house; they will be still [always] praising thee" (Psa. 84:4). It has been pointed out that in heaven praise is so important that it constitutes the total occupation of a certain order of beings (Rev. 4:8). God gave to King David such a revelation of the importance and power of praise upon earth that, following the heavenly pattern, he set aside and dedicated an army of four thousand Levites whose sole occupation was to praise the Lord (1 Chron. 23:5). They did nothing else. One of the last official acts of King David before his death was the organization of a formal program of praise. Each morning and each evening a contingent of these four thousand Levites engaged in this service. "And to stand every morning to thank and praise the Lord, and likewise at evening" (1 Chron. 23:30 *NS*). To the shame and defeat of the Church, the significance of the massive praise content of the Word has been largely overlooked.[2]

Praise as a Way of Life

To be most effective, then, praise must be massive, continuous, a fixed habit, a full-time occupation, a diligently pursued vocation, a total way of life. This principle is emphasized in Psalm 57:7: "My heart is *fixed,* O God, my heart is fixed; I *will* sing and give praise." This suggests a premeditated and predetermined habit of praise. "My heart is FIXED." This kind of praise depends on something more than temporary euphoria. We are told that at the very moment of the writing of this psalm David was a fugitive from the wrath of Saul. His praise was upon principle, not impulse. It was based upon something more than fluctuating circumstances or ephemeral emotional states. It was praise which had penetrated and permeated the warp and woof of his being. It was praise which had become a full-time occupation, reflecting the pattern of continuous, unceasing praise in the celestial sphere.

Praise for All Things

This order of praise is not always easy, for it does not come spontaneously. It is no problem to praise in prosperity. It is not difficult to praise when circumstances seem favorable. It is natural to praise for "good" things. It is normal to be thankful for and rejoice in success, prosperity, good health, and fame. But David was praising while his life was in jeopardy. The Apostle Paul says that one is to "give thanks *always* for *all things*" (Eph. 5:20). This, therefore, must include things that are painful, humiliating, and that even seem disastrous.

The Basis for Unceasing Praise

The self-evident truth which inspires this unceasing praise is the character and integrity of God Himself. If Satan had been successful in his attempt to dethrone the Most High, almighty selfishness instead of Almighty Love would be upon the throne of the universe. If Satan had triumphed, all life would have been at the mercy of almighty malevolence. Instead of hell with boundaries, the entire universe would be hell. But, praise God, Satan lost. Today there is "a heart at the heart of the universe." "The hands that were pierced do move the wheels of human history and mold the circumstances of individual lives" (Maclaren). As David said in Psalm 31:15: "My times are in thy hand." *Because Almighty Love is supreme, all who are in its embrace are kept safely and "the wicked one toucheth him not"* (1 John 5:18). *Nothing that is intrinsically evil can possibly reach a child of God because Almighty Love works all things, both "evil" and "good," to the ultimate benefit of the beloved. This includes all that seems most evil, even the mistakes of the trusting child of God.*

Praise as a Sacrifice

How can one offer this kind of praise? Hebrews 13:15 gives us the key: "By him, therefore, let us offer the *sacrifice* of praise to God *continually,* that is, the fruit of our lips." What is meant by "the sacrifice of praise?" A sacrifice calls for death. In the Old Testament ritual it was an animal that died. But in the "sacrifice of praise" it is the personal ego which must be slain. *One must sacrifice his own judgment, his own opinion, his own evaluation of what is right and good, and "praise God always for all things" including "good," "bad," and "indifferent."* "The fruit of the lips." This means that the sacrifice of praise is incomplete until it is expressed.

Almost everyone has been or is the victim of circumstances and situations which, to his judgment, seem unfortunate, tragic, even calamitous; conditions in which he can see no good, only evil. It is humanly impossible to see how any beneficial purpose can be served by them. It is then that one offers "the sacrifice of praise." *The only time one can offer this "sacrifice of praise" is when things seem to be going wrong,* for it is only then that he is called upon to die to his own opinions, choices, and judgment.

The Faith Which Supports Unceasing Praise

In offering the "sacrifice of praise" one embraces the faith that God is both benevolent and supreme, the faith that can "be still and know that [He is] God" (Psa. 46:10). This faith knows that there is nothing at loose ends in the universe. It knows that Satan can never slip up on the "blind side" of God for He is the *all*-seeing One. This faith is certain that, since God is supreme, He has the skill to outwit Satan, not in some, but in *all* crises and dilemmas which Satan's evil genius contrives and attempts to promote.

Praise Removes the "Evil" From Any Situation

Since all the "evil" in any situation is always because of Satan's active presence and agency, and since he is allergic to praise, therefore victorious, triumphant, massive praise casts him out, just as it did from heaven. When Satan is cast out, the evil vanishes. Even if the circumstances are not changed, the evil is removed, its fangs are drawn, its poison is extracted. The idea that "praise *always* changes circumstances" is a mistake. It may not always change circumstances, but it *will* change the *person. Since the root of all our problems is the unsanctified ego, inside change may be more important than changed circumstances.* Therefore, in offering the "sacrifice of praise" one accepts the position that nothing but "good" can come to the child of God, no matter how "evil" it may seem. Knowing that "all things," including apparent "evil," are certainly working for one's good, is ample basis for a life of continual praise.

Praising for Cancer

Amy Carmichael has said that the eternal essence of a thing or a circumstance is not in the thing itself but in one's reaction to it. The distressing situation will pass, but one's reaction to it results in a permanent moral and spiritual deposit in the character. Satan intends that adversity shall drive one away from God, causing him to sit in judgment upon Him, to question His motives, His goodness, and justice. Satan slanders God by suggesting that God has mistreated one, and that if He was really all good and all powerful He would never allow this sorrow or calamity to come to any of His children.

When one heeds and accepts Satan's suggestions and begins to doubt and accuse God of unfaithfulness and perfidy, then he begins to rebel against God, and his character deteriorates. This is what Satan intends; and when he succeeds, he has won.

When, instead, one allows the misfortune, affliction, or sorrow to drive him to God, the effect is just the opposite. Accepting the seeming misfortune as from the hand of an all-wise, all-loving and all-powerful God, who always works all things together for the good of the beloved, and praising Him that nothing intrinsically evil can ever come to one of His children, *is a reaction which strengthens and reinforces all that is best and most godlike in character.* With this reaction God's purpose is achieved and Satan has lost. *The adversity has left the individual stronger in faith, courage, and knowledge of God.* This is why a woman who had been brought back to God by a malignancy could triumphantly say, "I have been richly blessed by cancer." It also illuminates Maclaren's exhortation: "Don't waste your sorrows," and Watchman Nee's assertion that one never learns anything new about God except through adversity.

A God who can take all "evil," even the mistakes and sins of a penitent child of God, and by the alchemy of His divine grace so transform them that they boomerang against Satan, enhance the character of the saint, and redound to the glory of God, is worthy of unceasing praise. A God with such a character is adequate basis for obedience to the exhortation, "Giving thanks always for all things in the name of our Lord Jesus Christ to God, even the Father" (Eph. 5:20 *ASV*).

> Ill that He blesses is our good,
> And unblest good is ill;
> And all is right which seems most wrong,
> If it be His sweet will.[3]

This is the basis for the faith that nothing intrinsically evil can come to a trusting child of God (Psa. 91:10).

Praise, the Secret of Faith Without Doubt

Mrs. Metcalf has voiced the conviction that thanks-giving and praise is the way to victory in *every* situation. This is a broad statement, but it is both logical and scriptural. Since Satan is the great hindrance to successful prayer, when he is bound and banished from a situation the answers come through without fail. After all, successful prayer is overcoming satanic opposition to the purposes of God. The missing element in prayer that does not prevail is *triumphant faith.* And the missing element in faith that does not triumph is *praise—perpetual, purposeful, aggressive praise.* Praise is the highest form of prayer because it combines petition with faith. *Praise is the spark plug of faith. It is the one thing needed to get faith airborne, enabling it to soar above the deadly miasma of doubt. Praise is the detergent which purifies faith and purges doubt from the heart.* The secret of answered prayer is faith without doubt (Mark 11:23). And the secret of faith without doubt is praise— continuous, massive, triumphant praise, praise that is a way of life. *This order of praise is the solution to the problem of living faith and successful prayer.*

NOTES

1. The power of praise is illustrated by an incident told by David Wilkerson in one of his books. According to the story, in the early part of his work among the gangs in New York City he encountered a group of boys on a street corner. As he approached them, there were signs that they were preparing to attack. Looking to the Lord for guidance, he continued his advance. At the instant they seemed poised to strike, David suddenly clapped his hands and shouted "Praise the Lord!" According to the account, the entire gang broke ranks and fled. The only plausible explanation for their action is that these boys were activated by evil spirits who panicked at the shout of praise.

But the story which, in my opinion, dwarfs all others in this category concerns a well-documented circumstance which took place near Holton, Ripley County, Indiana. It was told me by an elderly woman at the close of a service where I had spoken on this subject. The incident had been related to her by her husband's cousin, who lived in the community and had personal knowledge of the details.

According to the account, an evangelist had come to the local church for a series of evangelistic services. In order to be alone for prayer and meditation, the minister went out into a nearby field. He did not know that a dangerous bull was in that area, until the attack was under way. When he saw the bull charging it was too late to reach safety. He did not know what to do. He thought he had come to his end. But just before the enraged animal reached him, he shouted "Praise the Lord." The bull halted in its tracks, immediately turned, and fled.

What is the explanation? The writer suggests that Satan sent evil spirits to enter this animal and incite him to attack this man of God in order to stop the revival effort. But the shouts of praise discomfited the evil spirits inhabiting this beast in the same way that the praises of the choir discomfited the evil spirits motivating Israel's foes.

2.   It is generally recognized that one of the fastest growing segments of the Christian communion is that group of churches and congregations which are of the Pentecostal persuasion. It is customary for Pentecostals to attribute this rapid expansion to their doctrinal distinctives and specifically to their emphasis upon glossolalia, or the speaking in tongues, as the initial evidence of the baptism with the Holy Ghost.

Many outside and some within the movement have their reservations upon this point. But whatever one's position may be, it cannot be denied that the Pentecostal groups have rediscovered, for this day and age, the importance and power of praise. To the order of public worship, including periods of congregational singing, public prayer, and a gospel message, they have added another coequal with these: a period of united worship and vocal praise. Almost universally, at some point in the service (usually preceding the spoken Word) time is given specifically for the purpose of worshiping and praising the Lord. At a given signal, usually by the pastor, the entire group raises hands to heaven and, with uplifted faces, enters into adoration and praise. This is not a subjective thing, an attempt to "work up" an ecstatic emotionalism for the sake of the thrill. But the objective thrust of the united praise and worship of Him who alone is worthy often results in an inundation of the Holy Spirit's presence — which is nothing short of heavenly, for it echoes the praises of the celestial throng around the throne.

It is the writer's considered judgment that it is this thoroughly scriptural program of *massive praise* which is responsible for the burgeoning growth of this movement, rather than its doctrinal distinctives. Regardless of one's position on the subject of tongues, there is nothing to hinder any group from adopting the scriptural practice of massive praise. The Church at large should sincerely repent of its failue to comprehend the overwhelming content of the Word on praise, and render due thanks to God for those instrumental in its rediscovery.

3.   NO SUCH THING AS BAD NEWS! Someone has said that there is no such thing as "bad news" for a Bible-believing Christian. They are just "new challenges to our faith." As we grow spiritually, God can trust us with bigger problems! This is an "obstacle race" we are traveling, from conversion to translation; and as we pray for and get answers to prayer for victory over the smaller obstacles which

Satan is allowed to put in our way, God permits somewhat larger ones to confront us — "God's hurdles," if you please, "on life's track." Who ever heard of an athlete, training for an obstacle race, pleading with his trainer to remove the obstacles? God has promised some very wonderful rewards for the "overcomers," and how can we ever be overcomers with nothing to overcome? Let us show all onlookers (to the glory of God) that we believe Romans 8:28 and Ephesians 1:11 when "bad news" is given to us, and immediately begin thanking God that He is "big" enough, "powerful" enough, and "loving" enough to take care of this new threat in a way that will bring still more glory to His Name *when we have overcome!* (From *Temple Times* — Emphasis mine).

9

ORGANIZED ACTION

Evening, and morning, and at noon, will I pray, and cry aloud, and he shall hear my voice (Psalm 55:17).

If the reading of this book does not inspire a well-organized program of prayer in both personal and group or church life, the work will have been in vain. *Satan does not care how many people read about prayer if only he can keep them from praying.* When a church is truly convinced that *"prayer is where the action is,"* that church will so construct its corporate activities that the prayer program will have the highest priority. Instead of leaving the prayer enterprise to be regulated by impulse, inclination, or blind chance, it will have the benefit of the best organizing talent, the most competent leadership, and the most sanctified dedication which the church affords. Unless a church is satisfied to merely operate an ecclesiastical treadmill, *prayer will become her main occupation.*

The effectiveness of the prayer program of a church will be in direct proportion to the depth of the individual prayer life of its members. Without a deep devotional life on the part of the participants, the group cannot muster great prayer power.

First Things First

Finding time for prayer is a matter of priorities. *All of us have the same amount of time in a twenty-four hour day.* One's use and management of time depends upon one's system of values. *Whatever one deems of greatest importance will have priority.* Almost everyone takes time to eat, sleep, and observe the ordinary demands of daily living. Most have the responsibility of a gainful occupation or profession. The duties and responsibilities of home-making and motherhood, in spite of all our modern conveniences, are most time-consuming. Even so, conscientious and efficient management of time will make possible a life of daily devotion and prayer that is deeply rewarding.

Organized Priorities

There are 168 hours in a week. After working 40 hours on the job, 128 remain. Allowing 56 hours for sleep still leaves 72. Counting 21 hours per week for meals reduces the balance to 51 hours. All of these activities seem to be irreducibly necessary. Taking from that balance a minimum of 1 hour per day for Scripture reading and prayer, one still has 44 hours a week for unanticipated and unprogrammed activities. This theoretical and hypo-thetical program does not apply to housewives and farmers, I know. It is only an attempt to illustrate that disciplined management of time and a proper system of priorities can make possible at least a minimal devotional life. *Those who are disabled or retired have the time and opportunity to make intercessory prayer the major activity of their lives.*

A Prayer Library

Each local church or group must decide the form and structure of its prayer program. However it *must* constitute the *main business* of the church, both individually and collectively. Every church should build a prayer library consisting of the best prayer classics. There are many good books on prayer but only a few classics. Those by E. M. Bounds are among the best. *Quiet Talks on Prayer* by S. D. Gordon, *The Life and Diary of David Brainerd, Praying Hyde, The Kneeling Christian* — these are only a few of the most valuable ones. These and others should be circulated so that the entire group will become faithful readers of these works.

Prayer Plan Hints

In any adequate prayer program, the midweek prayer service is only a starter. This should be supplemented by cottage prayer meetings where the time is conscientiously given to prayer. A variety of gatherings such as ladies' prayer cells, men's prayer groups, young adult prayer circles, and high school prayer bands at noon are all possibilities. Some of these may function as early-morning prayer meetings before work, as mid-morning assemblies, lunchtime gatherings, etc., as well as all-nights or half-nights of prayer. If it is not feasible to have an all-night of prayer each week, one night a month is suggested as a beginning. It is better to begin with a small program that can be maintained and increased than to plunge into too heavy a program and flounder. The program may include one day of fasting and prayer weekly, or at least monthly. Almost any church can have a prayer chain once a week or once a month, in which a different person prays each hour of the day and/or night. Some congregations may be large enough to maintain a continuous chain of prayer around the clock throughout the entire week. The Moravians, who had their beginning under Count Zinzendorf, carried on a chain of prayer day and night which continued uninterrupted for 100 years. This was the beginning of the modern missionary movement.

An effective prayer program may include a prayer list, compiled and continuously serviced by the pastor, and made available to each member of the praying contingent.

Each church must find God's leading for its own peculiar and particular situation and circumstance. *Remember: Only so much as is accomplished by prayer and faith is authentic and valid.* All else is frustratingly false and deceptive, mere shadow boxing and treadmill walking.

PRAYER IS WHERE THE ACTION IS; therefore, MOBILIZE FOR PRAYER.

To those individuals and churches who desire an organized systematic program of prayer for daily use, the author suggests "The 2959 Plan" devised by Peter Lord, pastor of the Park Avenue Baptist Church of Titusville, Florida. An explanatory tape accompanies the book. Send all inquiries to:

> Peter Lord
> Park Avenue Baptist Church
> 2600 Park Avenue
> Titusville, Florida 32780.

Perhaps the most significant prayer movement in the world today is sponsored by CHANGE THE WORLD MINISTRIES. Currently CTWM conducts SCHOOLS OF PRAYER in major cities throughout the United States. For further information on how you can participate in a Change the World School of Prayer in a city near you, write to:

> CHANGE THE WORLD MINISTRIES
> P. O. Box 5838
> Mission Hills, CA 91345

The following material is included by special request of the author:

APPENDIX: PRACTICAL PRAYING

by Dick Eastman, Director
Change the World Ministries
P. O. Box 5838, Mission Hills, CA 91345

"'Prayer is the mightiest force in the universe," wrote an atomic scientist several years ago. No statement could be more accurate.

Not only does prayer bring the individual into union with the Ruler of the Universe, but it releases His power into a world that desperately needs changing. This is why Change the World Ministries is carrying out the most intense effort to mobilize and train prayer warriors in the history of the Christan Church, including organizing and conducting Change the World Schools of Prayer. You, too, can join this force. But you must not wait another day to get involved.

Sadly, many Christians fail to join the ranks of those pray-ers we call "world changers" because they have never learned to make their prayer life practical. This is why we have added this appendix to Paul Billheimer's provocative book.

To pray in a practical, systematic manner, the prayer warrior needs two things: something to pray about during his or her prayer time, and a quiet place to pray, a place where uninterrupted intercession can be offered for needs of the world. To make your prayer more practical, consider these two areas of thought.

How to Pray

God gives you 96 fifteen-minute time periods every day. Will you give God at least one or two of these time periods in prayer for your loved ones, friends, and the world? Some people do not respond because they lack a workable method in their prayer life. Some say, "I let the Holy Spirit lead," and when asked how much prayer the Holy Spirit led them into during the last week, they blush with embarrassment. Indeed, why must we wait for a call today when God's Word cries out to all generations: "Pray without ceasing" (I Thess. 5:17). Thus we have a constant call, and to be obedient to that call, we must answer. That is why we offer the reader several hints on how to pray . . . .

First, divide your fifteen-minute time period into three periods. The first five-minute period could be given to praise, adoration and worship of the Lord. Take time to love God because He is God. Remember, the way to enter the gates of heaven is thanksgiving and praise (Ps. 100). After this you will be ready to pray for other needs.

Second, take five minutes to pray for needs that are close to you. This could mean prayer for family concerns as well as for your local area, including your church and pastor. You will be surprised how much can be included in a five-minute prayer time.

Finally, pray for specific countries of the world. (Change the World Ministries has Prayer Maps available on request to all interested prayer warriors. These maps show the location of all countries as well as their names.) Since there are 210 separate geographical areas we call countries, to name all 210 in five minutes would mean mere mention of each country. Our suggestion is to either extend your prayer time or divide the 210 countries into thirty countries each, daily lifting thirty of the countries before God. Thus, every seven days you will be praying for the whole world.

But what can we pray about concerning these many obscure places? For one thing, most certainly follow the command of Jesus to pray that the Lord of harvest will send forth laborers into the harvest (Matt. 9:38). We should also ask God for the conversion of souls in each country, since His Word declares, "Ask of me and I will give you the heathen for thine inheritance . . ." (Ps. 2:8). Further, pray that God will bless the efforts of distributing Gospel literature and the witness of a personal testimony in that specific geographic area. A sample prayer might be as follows: "Oh God, I lift before you Indonesia. Please send forth laborers into the harvest of Indonesia, and bless those ministers presently carrying forth the Gospel throughout Indonesia. Place a special anointing on the daily efforts of your precious servants as they attempt to reach every home with the Gospel in many villages today."

The above prayer requires less than twenty seconds and yet calls to God on behalf of that nation. Even if the prayer warrior only mentions the country in but a passing prayer, God will honor such intercession. Of course, in all of this we must covet the precious leading of God's Spirit. He will often prompt us to stop and pray more carefully for a certain country. And remember, when calling on God in behalf of Communist or Moslem nations, be sure to ask God that leaders in the highest levels of these governments will experience changes of attitude so doors will open for an anointed systematic distribution of the Gospel to all the people of these countries.

In fact, Paul challenged his co-worker, young Timothy, to pray especially for "all who are in authority" (I Tim. 2:2). This includes kings, presidents, premiers, and even dictators. We are to ask God to move the hearts of these men in such a way that doors open in their countries for the spread of the Gospel. To aid you in this unique prayer focus, we have prepared a special listing of all kings and presidents for every country in the world. This is one of the most unusual prayer lists being circulated by any missionary organization in the world. And if you use it every day, your contribution to world evangelism will be truly "world changing." So be sure to write our office and request these free prayer helps. Please list those helps you desire. Items available include: the Prayer Map, a list of kings and presidents, and a special pamphlet entitled, "15 Ways to Make Your Prayer Life More Meaningful."

Where to Pray

Following several years in which God showed this author the impact and value of prayer, he was jolted one night by a startling vision of a prayer center where college-age youth could come from across the country to offer God a gift of time set aside as an offering of intercession. During the year of their commitment these dedicated youth would pray at least two hours a day, praying in specific, assigned time periods so that prayer would never stop day or night at that center. The specific room where these young people would pray was to be called "The Gap," based on God's words to Ezekiel, "I sought for a man among them that should make up the hedge and stand in the gap before me for the land . . ." (Ezek. 22:30). Six months after the evening of this challenging vision, God gave us our prayer center. For years prayer has continued day and night in "The Gap" at this prayer center. Many miracles have resulted from this prayer, not the least of which is the spreading of the "gap concept." Today, hundreds of families, churches and colleges have begun a gap ministry by setting aside a specific place called "The Gap," where people can pray for the needs of the world.

To my knowledge, the first couple to ever begin a

gap ministry in the home as the result of hearing about our prayer center was from a Baptist background. Since that time people from many denominations have written us saying, "Add us to your 'gap' list! We've begun a family prayer ministry in our home."

My wife Dee and I have started our own family gap ministry. We have a special family prayer chapel built in our back yard where we can go individually or together for prayer and devotions. It has revolutionized my personal prayer life. Each day I pray for the countries of the world in our gap. What a thrill to hear our two young daughters, Dena and Ginger, beg us to go to "the gap" to hear about Jesus and pray. They invariably want me to tell them about different countries of the world on the globe, one of the few objects of furniture in our gap.

To begin a gap ministry, one must simply set aside a closet or spare room for a place of prayer. Our family saved the necessary money to put down an inexpensive piece of carpet and to panel the walls of our gap so the atmosphere would be conducive to quiet prayer. Of course, the most important thing is a special place reserved just for prayer. Our gap is not a sewing room, den, or office that doubles as a prayer chapel. Every family member knows it is our special "Gethsemane" where we can retreat to be alone with our Lord. I challenge the reader to start a gap ministry soon and register your gap ministry with our Office of Intercession gap list.

Direct all requests for further information to:

Change the World Ministries
P. O. Box 5838
Mission Hills, CA 91345.